Chapter 1
DROP YOUR CARE

CONTENTS

FOREWORD

As I was preparing for a sermon dealing with faith, God directed me to a very familiar Bible story about a blind beggar by the name of Bartimaeus. Not only was I directed to this awesome story found in Mark 10, but God began to unravel some amazing revelations regarding this story. It's one of those stories (like many in the Bible) where God speaks to you in fresh and new ways every time you read it. For me, this story spoke not only of faith, but also of courage and a commitment to no longer settle for the way things are, but rather chase after what they could be.

In your hands is a 21 Day Devotional inspired by the awesome story of a blind beggar. This "Drop It" Devotional will challenge and inspire you to Cut the Strings to the Things That Control Your Life.

The devotional is broken down into 3 Chapters over 21 days. Each day is designed to be consumed separately. Feel free to skip a day or so, or maybe even take a break on the weekends. The most important aspect of this devotional is to make sure that you are honest with yourself and that you dive into the content with a commitment to grow. Each day is designed to be completed with a morning section and an evening section; however, you could complete each day in one sitting if you desire. Again, it's not about when you engage the content; it's about how you engage it.

The Word will be your daily Scripture and the **Daily Dose** will be the daily devotional content.

The **Key Thought** section is meant to help you focus on a main daily concept, quote, idea or thought to increase your faith to the level needed to accomplish the dreams God put inside you. Each day will also include **Questions For Reflection**, **PM** section and a **Notes** section to get you thinking actively about your faith, yourself, others and God.

The daily Scripture reading, thoughts and questions are designed to help you interact with what God says about the subject matter in each chapter. Learning to focus on what God says about each concept will give you the faith, confidence and courage to begin obeying what He asks of you and following what He inspires in you. Take advantage of the Notes section to jot down your daily thoughts, "aha's," ideas and momentum-building moments. Make sure to come back to the notes section periodically and engage with it, like you would with a journal or the margins in your Bible.

Just like Bartimaeus, you will begin putting these faith concepts and principles into practice. We need to always be reminded what it truly means to be a doer of the Word and not just hearers. (Or in this case, not just readers.)

It's time for you to take control of your life, ignite your faith and no longer be a puppet to the things that are distracting you from your purpose.

It's Time to "**DROP IT!**"

Blind Bartimaeus Receives His Sight

46 Then they came to Jericho. As Jesus and his disciples, together with a large crowd, were leaving the city, a blind man, Bartimaeus, was sitting by the roadside begging.

47 When he heard that it was Jesus of Nazareth, he began to shout, "Jesus, Son of David, have mercy on me!"

48 Many rebuked him and told him to be quiet, but he shouted all the more, "Son of David, have mercy on me!"

49 Jesus stopped and said, "Call him." So they called to the blind man, "Cheer up! On your feet! He's calling you."

50 Throwing his cloak aside, he jumped to his feet and came to Jesus.

51 "What do you want me to do for you?" Jesus asked him.

The blind man said, "Rabbi, I want to see."

52 "Go," said Jesus, "your faith has healed you." Immediately he received his sight and followed Jesus along the road.

- Mark 10:46-52

Day 1:
PILGRIMAGE

The Word

Then they came to Jericho. As Jesus and his disciples, together with a large crowd, were leaving the city, a blind man, Bartimaeus, was sitting by the roadside begging. - Mark 10:46

I lift up my eyes to the mountains—where does my help come from?
My help comes from the Lord, the Maker of heaven and earth.
He will not let your foot slip—he who watches over you will not slumber;
indeed, he who watches over Israel will neither slumber nor sleep.
The Lord watches over you—the Lord is your shade at your right hand;
the sun will not harm you by day, nor the moon by night.
The Lord will keep you from all harm—he will watch over your life;
the Lord will watch over your coming and going both now and forevermore. - Psalm 121

Daily Dose

During the days of Jesus' life, devout Jewish men would make three pilgrimages to the Holy City each year for the major festivals of Passover, Pentecost and Tabernacles. Jesus and his disciples would set out on pilgrimages together, 120 miles one way from Nazareth to Jerusalem.

Nazareth is in Galilee, a stunning landscape full of volcanic hills and fertile farmlands with a climate cooler than any other part of Palestine. The most direct route to Jerusalem would be through Samaria, but this would be avoided. In contrast to Galilee, Samaria was often seen as unwelcoming—a dry, barren, hot landscape—but also a place to be avoided at all costs due to heavy crime and cultural tensions. Adding as much as 30 miles to their pilgrimage, Galilean Jews would avoid the difficulty of Samaria and stay alongside the Eastern banks of the Jordan River.

Like the tributaries that fed the winding river towards Jerusalem, the crowds would begin to swell as people made their way from their own towns and villages. Though it was required by the law, it was not seen as an obligation but a joy to journey to the Holy City as one of God's faithful people. Many of the Northern tribes would find themselves together in Jericho, a common stopover just about 15 miles (a day's journey) from Jerusalem.

Though Jericho is on the edge of the wilderness, it was considered a pleasant and desirable place with a warm winter climate, several sources of fresh water and a prominent location along major travel routes. Several times in the Old Testament it is referred to as the "City of Palm Trees" and its name has been connected to descriptions of the sweet smell of the region from the fruits and spices that grow in abundance. Additionally, Jericho had always held a special place in the hearts of the Jewish people as the first place of victory in the Promised Land, as well as the headquarters of the prophet Elisha and at one point the home of the "company of the prophets."

But Jesus and his disciples knew as they woke up on the last day of their journey that it would be their most difficult. An incredibly steep road led them out of Jericho to Jerusalem. God's faithful, now tens of thousands in number, would journey together during the arduous climb in a prayerful and worshipful way, reciting and singing the Songs of Ascent, chapters 120-134 of the Psalms. One of the most famous of these songs, Psalm 121, opens our mind's eye to imagine the historical pilgrimage, a people expressing their devotion, a people enduring a difficult climb, a people almost home to their God:

> **I lift up my eyes to the mountains–where does my help come from?**
> **My help comes from the Lord, the Maker of heaven and earth.**
> **He will not let your foot slip–he who watches over you will not slumber;**
> **indeed, he who watches over Israel will neither slumber nor sleep.**
> **The Lord watches over you–the Lord is your shade at your right hand;**
> **the sun will not harm you by day, nor the moon by night.**
> **The Lord will keep you from all harm–he will watch over your life;**
> **the Lord will watch over your coming and going both now and forevermore. - Psalm 121**

The annual pilgrimages were a rhythm of life for God's ancient people, and they would go out of their way to sustain a rhythm that was as comfortable and as easy as possible. They would stay in the beautiful country, avoid people who were different from them, follow the river, stay close to the familiar landmarks and travel with a buddy. They even controlled the difficulty, waiting until the last possible moment to face the mountains and the arduous climb towards their goal. And in the midst of that climb, they would cling to their Scriptures, recognizing the need for God's help and deliverance, his ever wakeful care and protection.

Are we any different today?

We like to be in a comfortable rhythm, stay in the beautiful country, avoid people different from us, follow the river, stay close to the familiar landmarks, and travel with our friends. We certainly like to control the difficulty and avoid the suffering, but when it comes, we finally blow the dust off that Bible.

A pilgrimage is any time in life when we are trying to get somewhere while staying focused on God, controlling the circumstances and avoiding the difficulty. Our destinations are often things like a job, a financial provision, a relationship, a healing or a reconciliation. But we cannot control our pilgrimage toward our spiritual destination any more than those around Jesus could control their pilgrimage towards Jerusalem. Weather, sickness, unexpected delays and detours could come at any time, even along their comfortable route. But even if the unexpected didn't happen, there was no way to avoid the climb at the end.

There are no shortcuts to pilgrimage. Sometimes we've got to go through something in order to get to something.

Even Bartimaeus was on his own difficult journey. With

no eyesight, he was destined to an existence that we all recognize: the broken record of the beggar looking for spare change. With the dust of traveler's feet on his lips, he would mouth the same words every day, watching those wealthy enough to travel pass through his town throughout the year, coming and going to the place of privilege. While all the people passing him were affluent enough to go on pilgrimage, he was stuck on a beggar's mat.

But Bartimaeus soon learns that Jesus is on pilgrimage. Isn't that odd? All the people around Jesus are on pilgrimage to meet with God, but God through Jesus is on a pilgrimage to meet with the people.

Jesus rolls up on Bartimaeus and not only do their paths cross, but their pilgrimages cross. It's an invitation to remind us all that we don't control our pilgrimage. God can insert Himself at any moment, whether we are comforted by the illusion that we control our lives or discomforted by the reality that we don't.

Key Thought
Sometimes you've got to go through something in order to get to something.

Questions for Reflection

What is the destination of the pilgrimage you are currently on? Are you more like the affluent crowds who are comforted by the illusion of control, or more like Blind Bartimaeus who is discomforted by his lack of control? What would it look like for you to embrace your own pilgrimage?

PM

Read the Songs of Ascent in Psalms 120-134 in one sitting and write all the answers you find to one question: What characteristics of God does this passage reveal?

For example, when reading Psalm 120, you may write God is my help, God is my shield, etc.

Notes

Day 2:
BLINDNESS

The Word

Then they came to Jericho. As Jesus and his disciples, together with a large crowd, were leaving the city, a blind man, Bartimaeus, was sitting by the roadside begging. - Mark 10:46

"Very truly I tell you, no one can see the kingdom of God unless they are born again." - John 3:3

"If the blind lead the blind, both will fall into a pit." - Matthew 15:14

"Then will the eyes of the blind be opened and the ears of the deaf unstopped. Then will the lame leap like a deer and the mute tongue shout for joy."
- Isaiah 35:5-6

Daily Dose

A blind beggar has positioned himself along a strategic point in the Jewish pilgrimage to Jerusalem. We don't know much about the blind man Bartimaeus, other than that he had been blind from birth and how incredibly skilled he was at begging! Think about it: what Bartimaeus would do is try to capture the hearts and the generosity of the Galilean Jews that were on this pilgrimage, so he would just sit there and beg. It's a pretty smart place to beg because people tend to feel more generous when they've been worshipping God. The law dictated that a disabled man in the ancient world was totally dependent on others for charity and for guidance and protection (Lev. 19:4). As this law would come to mind, the people who had means to make a pilgrimage would feel a compulsion to give; they would feel pity, empathy, compassion and even an obligation to the rule of law. So Bartimaeus is a smart guy and it's safe to say he made bank during the three major pilgrimages. Sure, he received other things – people would give him advice, talk to him, listen to his story, and share things with him. But Bartimaeus was doing what he was doing in that place for money, and he made plenty of it.

But all that is on the surface of the story. Yes, he is blind and begging, and yes, people are helping him, and yes, Jesus is going to really heal him. But this story is not about a single man born with blindness. Instead, it is about every man and woman born with spiritual blindness. Our spiritual need is greater than our physical circumstances.

Spiritual blindness is a parable for the inability to see Jesus Christ for who he really is and what he can really do for us. Bartimaeus is the only physically blind man in this story but almost everyone else is spiritually blind—they do not recognize who Jesus really is and they do not understand what Jesus can really do for them. Bartimaeus wants his sight restored and Jesus is going to do it, but he will do it in a way that teaches everyone about spiritual blindness. Jesus often talked about blindness as a figurative way of defining the lost and hopeless condition of sinful people–an inability to see God in creation or in the proclaimed truth of the Gospel. In one of his most famous teachings on spiritual blindness, Jesus charged the Pharisees with unbelief that made them "blind guides of the blind" (Mt 15:14; 23:16). This stunning charge by Jesus was simply a carryover from the Old Testament.

Moses spoke of Israel's apostasy as "blindness" (Dt 29:4); Isaiah called it "dim eyes" (Is 6:10 NASB), and there was a clear belief that one day when the Messiah would come, he would heal people of blindness. But to press even a bit further, spiritual blindness is related to "hardness of heart" (Mk 8:17-18; Eph. 4:17-18) and is understood as the judgment of God both upon unbelievers (Rom 1:20-21) and upon Israel (Is 29:10; Rom 11:7-8). According to Paul, it is also the work of Satan, who "has blinded the minds of the unbelievers" (2 Cor. 4:4).

Spiritual blindness is when we don't see Jesus for who he is, especially his ability to heal us. Spiritual blindness happens when our hearts become hardened to him. Like a cataract over our spiritual eyes, bitterness, rebellion or pride can keep us from seeing God clearly. And to top it all off, the whole time we've got an enemy who is working to keep us blinded as well.

But thanks be to God who gives us a special gift of God's grace through the "new birth" (Jn. 3:3) and by seeing "the light of the gospel of the glory of Christ" (2 Cor. 4:4).

So here's the point: the Pharisees weren't willing to do anything different. They weren't willing to ask the difficult questions like "how have I hardened my heart?" or "how has what I've been doing blinded me from seeing and experiencing God's best for my life?"

Jesus would have healed any of them spiritually in the same way he will heal Bartimaeus. But we cannot be made new unless we do some things differently.

Speaking of being blind and needing to do some things differently, that would describe me when it comes to my eyeglasses. I'm at that age where it's harder and harder to see things up close without my glasses. In an attempt to avoid the dreaded bifocals, I continue to wait and self-adjust. My optometrist continues to remind me that pretty soon my arms are not going to be long enough to self-adjust.

The same principle holds true in life. Your power for self-adjustment is limited. If you want to see God differently, you have to do things differently. You're not going to see what God has for you unless you stop self-adjusting and allow him to give you what you need for new and perfect vision.

Key Thought
If you want to see things differently, then you have to do things differently.

Questions for Reflection

What examples in your life would diagnose your blindness? Who might you ask to help you "see?" What adjustments, tweaks and changes do you need to make in your life?

PM

There are eleven Scriptures referenced in the devotional for this day. Take the time to read each of these Scriptures and ask the LORD to give you insight into how each one speaks directly to your situation right now in life.

Notes

Day 3:
ON THE WAY

The Word

Then they came to Jericho. As Jesus and his disciples, together with a large crowd, were leaving the city, a blind man, Bartimaeus, was sitting by the roadside begging. - Mark 10:46

Daily Dose

Notice this little detail to the text, which is even more vivid in the original language: Bartimaeus is seated "by the way." This is important because Bartimaeus, when we first meet him, is not "on the way" with Jesus.

The disciples, together with the large crowd, are all leaving the city and on the way with Jesus. The "way" in this case is the physical pilgrimage to Jerusalem, and Bartimaeus isn't on that way. He is isolated; they are together. He is outcast; they are insiders. He is sitting; they are moving. Bartimaeus is stuck in a rut; the people are on pilgrimage.

Why is Bartimaeus stuck?

Well, there were clearly some cultural reasons. The book of Leviticus told Bartimaeus that being a beggar was now his place in society and he was to depend on everyone else. There was also the spiritual stigma of blindness, where people believed you had been cursed by God because of something you or your parents had done. Finally, there was the obvious challenge of being physically impaired in the first century–no social systems to help you, no real easy ways to communicate, usually abandoned. Bartimaeus is stuck in his fears, limitations, and blindness. He is totally dependent upon the mercy of others just to survive and get by from day to day. He is small, insignificant and virtually invisible to the crowds around him. He is hopeless.

Life "by the way" instead of "on the way" with Jesus is no different for us today. We feel isolated, outcast and stuck. We too feel stuck in fear of our limitations, left at the mercy of others to just survive and get by. Many of us feel small, insignificant and virtually invisible to everyone else around us. Most people feel hopeless.

Bartimaeus had enough courage to drop his care, even though everything about his situation defined him by his beggary, his condition, his limitations and fears. But Bartimaeus' story is in the Bible because he has 21 seconds of insane faith. He was audacious enough to say, "You know what? I'm not defined by my blindness and I don't have to just sit here. I have heard enough about Jesus to think maybe he could do something about my situation. Even if he can't, what do I have to lose?"

Bartimaeus drops his care of what others think in favor of following Jesus. He's not going to hold onto the excuse of his condition but rather try to get "on the way" with the one he believes can radically alter his condition.

Like it was for Bartimaeus, it's easy for us to pick up excuses instead of picking up an unmarked trail. Excuses are easily recited, they incite compassion and pity from others, and if we use them long enough, we buy into our own negative press. This makes us, like Bartimaeus, passive, afraid to act, unsure of how others are going to react, or even paralyzed by our fear of rejection or failure. Ring any bells?

It's time to stop making excuses.

I remember this poem about excuses that we used to have to recite while I was in college and pledging Alpha Phi Alpha Fraternity Inc. Alpha men were distinguished men; they were go-getters, they were achievers and they didn't make excuses. Even Martin Luther King, Jr. was an Alpha. The poem was short and sweet and I still remember it today, some 23 years later:

Excuses tools of incompetence,
Used to build monuments of nothingness,
Those who use them
Seldom amount to anything.
Excuses. Excuses.

The words of that poem still ring true in my life and your life.

Last year you said "Next year," last month you said "Next month," last week you said "Next week" and yesterday you said today. No more excuses.

Key Thought

Bartimaeus drops his care of what the "Large Crowd" thought about him in favor of following Jesus. He's not going to hold onto the excuse of his condition and caring about what people think, but rather reach out to the one he believes can radically alter his condition.

Questions for Reflection

In what area of your life are you sitting on the sidelines, waiting for someone to come along and give you a handout?

What are you willing to give up in order to have your condition erased?

PM

Get together with a friend or family member whom you know loves you and will be honest with you. Ask them one question: Where do you think I'm stuck right now?

Notes

Day 4:
HATERS

The Word

Then they came to Jericho. As Jesus and his disciples, together with a large crowd, were leaving the city, a blind man, Bartimaeus, was sitting by the roadside begging.
When he heard that it was Jesus of Nazareth, he began to shout, "Jesus, Son of David, have mercy on me!"
Many rebuked him and told him to be quiet, but he shouted all the more, "Son of David, have mercy on me!" - Mark 10:46-48

Be alert and of sober mind. Your enemy the devil prowls around like a roaring lion looking for someone to devour. - 1 Peter 5:8

The weeds are the people of the evil one, and the enemy who sows them is the devil. - Matthew 13:38-39

Daily Dose

You've got a Hater and you've got haters, and if you haven't learned this yet, only one of them can really affect you.

Haters are people who are against you. They discourage your dreams, disrupt your progress and detour you from God's best. Haters are going to hate, be negative and try to detour you from your destiny because that's what they do.

They also like to throw shade. According to the handy

dandy Urban Dictionary, **_throwing shade_** is defined as _acting in a casual or disrespectful manner towards someone_. It's a new way of talking about insult, hating, disparaging comments, snide remarks at or towards someone in an overt or sly manner.

Don't view shade as a negative; sometimes you have to wear it as a badge of honor. My pastor always says, "If you are looking for the leader making a difference, look for the one with the arrows in his back." I like to say it this way, **"People only throw shade on things that are hot**." You see, the hotter, better, faster and greater you become, the more shade is gonna get thrown.

But even though haters can throw shade, critique you or act as an obstacle, they aren't really the problem. God teaches us clearly that the real problem, the real Hater, is Satan, the enemy of our souls. One of his most common tactics is to use other people to keep you from the life God has for you. His tactics are to use other people to discourage, disrupt and detour you; he throws in confusion, temptation and a few surprises too.

Here's a secret to the enemy: he leaves you alone in proportion to how you are doing. The worse we are, the more he ignores us—he's already had some success and victory over us, so why bother? He has to turn his attention to those who are succeeding and doing well. You see, the better you are doing, the more success you are having, the greater your accomplishments, the more positive impact you are making for the Kingdom Of God, the harsher the enemy's tactics will become. In other words, as you reach new levels, you get new

Devils.

Now our guy Bartimaeus isn't really achieving much. So it doesn't seem like the devil is really in his business. But man, is the crowd around him throwing shade, and that is a tool of the enemy! Satan doesn't want people to see Jesus for who he really is, so he is throwing everything he's got at this poor blind man just to stop the healing in its tracks.

As Bartimaeus began to cry out for help, it says: "Many rebuked him and told him to be quiet, but he shouted all the more, 'Son of David, have mercy on me!'" They were yelling at him and telling him to be quiet and saying that Jesus didn't want to hear from him.

When the haters started throwing shade, telling Bartimaeus how unimportant he was and reminding him that he had issues, the more Bartimaeus began to yell and turn up the heat. He wouldn't be silenced, drowned out, discouraged, disrupted or detoured by the crowd.

You see, he wasn't worried about what the crowd thought, because he knew what he needed, and he had enough faith to see his healing on the other side. Bartimaeus was basically saying, "Yes, I may have issues, but I'm about to connect with the one that has ability to cancel my subscription."

If you want to see and live what God has for you, sometimes you have to do what a good orchestra conductor does: turn your back to the crowd. As long as you're looking at the crowd, you can't see where you need to go and where you want be. If you are always living your life through the thoughts and expectations of others, you will constantly find yourself in situations where you have no control over the win.

The Lord wants you to stand up and shout in the midst of your haters, but you've got to turn your back to them, quit listening, and not get discouraged, disrupted or detoured by the crowd. The crowd will never go away–the enemy will always throw shade your way–but that's a game you cannot play. You have to ignore it, be the conductor and play your music.

Key Thought
As you reach new levels, you get new Devils.

Questions for Reflection

How have you experienced the crowd throwing shade at you recently? How have you seen the enemy's tactics in your life?

PM

Write down some haters in your life that you need to ignore. What tangible things can you do to silence their voice in your life? It's possible, but you'll need to silence your own voice in this exercise!

Notes

Day 5:
WHY DO YOU WORRY?

The Word

Then they came to Jericho. As Jesus and his disciples, together with a large crowd, were leaving the city, a blind man, Bartimaeus, was sitting by the roadside begging. When he heard that it was Jesus of Nazareth, he began to shout, "Jesus, Son of David, have mercy on me!" Many rebuked him and told him to be quiet, but he shouted all the more, "Son of David, have mercy on me!" - Mark 10:46-48

"Therefore I tell you, do not worry about your life, what you will eat or drink; or about your body, what you will wear. Is not life more than food, and the body more than clothes? Look at the birds of the air; they do not sow or reap or store away in barns, and yet your heavenly Father feeds them. Are you not much more valuable than they? Can any one of you by worrying add a single hour to your life?

"And why do you worry about clothes? See how the flowers of the field grow. They do not labor or spin. Yet I tell you that not even Solomon in all his splendor was dressed like one of these. If that is how God clothes the grass of the field, which is here today and tomorrow is thrown into the fire, will he not much more clothe you– you of little faith? So do not worry, saying, 'What shall we eat?' or 'What shall we drink?' or 'What shall we wear?' For the pagans run after all these things, and your heavenly Father knows that you need them. But seek first his kingdom and his righteousness, and all these things will be given to you as well. Therefore do not worry

about tomorrow, for tomorrow will worry about itself. Each day has enough trouble of its own. - Matthew 6:25-34

Daily Dose

Yesterday we talked about the haters who throw shade. Inevitably, that shade is going to affect us, because we are obsessed with what people think. We may not be begging for money, but we are begging for comments, likes, views and affirmation. We do this even though we know it's not productive and can clearly see in the above Scripture where Jesus teaches that we aren't supposed to worry about anything. I know lots of Christians who follow the rules like good boys and girls, but will worry up a storm, particularly when it comes to worrying about what others think.

Maybe you are in college right now and majoring in a subject not because it is what you want, but because it's what your parents want. Maybe you are in a relationship that you know is not God's best, but you stay because you are worried about what your partner will say if you break up. Maybe you aren't spending time with your family because you are worried about what people at work think. Maybe instead of enjoying your kids' silliness in a restaurant, you yell at them because you are worried about what other patrons think. From driving a car that you can't afford to grabbing Starbucks on a daily basis, maybe you spend money you don't have–all because you're worried about what people think.

But if you worry and focus on what people think, guess

what happens? You become blind to what God thinks. When that happens, you are blind to hope, blind to the future, blind to what success even looks like. The more you settle for mediocrity, the more difficult it becomes to know what genius looks like. You will stumble and grope in the darkness, trying to hit the moving target of the happiness of others.

So how do you know what God thinks about you? Who does he say that you are? You may be surprised to know this, but God has a lot to say about what he thinks about you–a whole Bible full. But if we could summarize it in the spirit of this 21 day devotional, here are 21 things that God says about you:

1. I am a child of God. John 1:12
2. I am a friend with God. John 15:15
3. I am not condemned by God. Romans 8:1
4. I am an heir with Christ. Romans 8:17
5. I have wisdom, righteousness and redemption, in Christ Jesus. 1 Corinthians 1:30
6. I am a new creation. 2 Corinthians 5:17
7. I am the righteousness of God. 2 Corinthians 5:21
8. I have been set free. Galatians 5:1
9. I have been blessed with every spiritual blessing. Ephesians 1:3
10. I am God's incredible work of art. Ephesians 2:10
11. I am chosen, holy, and blameless before God. Ephesians 1:4
12. I am redeemed and forgiven by the grace of God. Ephesians 1:7
13. I am seated in the heavenly places with Christ. Ephesians 2:10
14. I have been brought near to God by the blood of

Christ. Ephesians 2:13

15. I am a member of Christ's body and a partaker of His promise. Ephesians 3:6
16. I have boldness and confident access to God through faith in Christ. Ephesians 3:12
17. I have been made complete in Christ. Colossians 2:10
18. I have been chosen by God, holy and dearly loved. Colossians 3:12
19. I am an overcomer in Christ Jesus. 1 John 5:4
20. I am a citizen of Heaven. Philippians 3:20
21. I Can Do All Things Through Christ. Philippians 4:13

That's a pretty good list to begin with and it should provide an incredible source of encouragement, confidence and faith.

If Bartimaeus was focused on what other people thought, he would have never met Jesus. Of course that would have meant he would have never been healed, but he also would have never experienced the truth of what God thought about him. I would have never preached a sermon on him, you would never have read this devotional, and the list goes on an on. One step of blind faith changed everything.

Through this healing, Jesus communicates the truth that he feels about Bartimaeus: he is precious, valued, loved, worthy of attention. Jesus treats Bartimaeus like a good father would treat a son of his who is sick or in need. Imagine an infant or toddler that wants to be picked up by their father. They simply reach their arms up towards their father, and the only natural response from the father is to pick them up. That's the same way our Heavenly father is. He picks us up when we activate our faith by reaching out our arms, calling on his name and getting up and on our feet and running towards Him.

In a world where everyone worries about their online image, their status among others, their bank accounts, their job titles and homes and cars, Christians should stand out as people who are peculiarly successful because they don't worry about it. The key to success is not reaching out and trying to get the approval of others, but instead reaching to a Heavenly Father that has already approved us.

Key Thought
The key to success is to STOP worrying about what people think and START worrying about what God thinks.

Questions for Reflection

What are your greatest worries right now? How does God's truth in the Bible speak to those worries? If you can't seem to come up with an answer to that on your own, ask a trusted Christian friend or mentor to help you discover God's truth related to those worries. If all else fails, Google it!

PM

Write down a list of the truths from the Bible that speak to your most common worries or simply circle some from the list of 21 provided in today's reading. Keep that list handy–on your phone, hanging in your home or office, etc. Pray and recite those truths daily!

Notes

Day 6:
SCREAM

The Word

> Then they came to Jericho. As Jesus and his disciples, together with a large crowd, were leaving the city, a blind man, Bartimaeus, was sitting by the roadside begging. When he heard that it was Jesus of Nazareth, he began to shout, "Jesus, Son of David, have mercy on me!" Many rebuked him and told him to be quiet, but he shouted all the more, "Son of David, have mercy on me!" - Mark 10:46-48

Daily Dose

Bartimaeus couldn't see, but he could hear, he could talk, and he could get up on his feet. When something is going wrong or not working right in our lives, our tendency is to focus on those things rather than the things that are working. If Bartimaeus had stayed focused on his blindness, he would just keep on begging and his miracle, would have passed him by. But he began to use his voice, and when the haters shouted him down, he turned his voice up and started shouting. And you know you can't shout very well while you are sitting down, so we are pretty certain that Bartimaeus stood up.

There was always a rope-line around Jesus that other people put there—a way of keeping people out. Lots of people found themselves on the other side of the man-made rope-line, but Jesus always welcomed those who jumped it—those who took fate in their own hands, who stood up and shouted when everyone said to be quiet.

There were other people who needed a miracle from Jesus who had to jump the rope-line. For one guy, the rope-line was a roof, and he needed his friends to carry him down a roof on a mat because he couldn't walk. For one woman, the rope-line was a crowd and her uncleanness and bleeding for 12 years, but she was so desperate she decided that if she could just touch Jesus' cloak, then she would be healed. But even those people found the one thing that could lead to their miracle and that's what they focused on. *If only I can jump the rope-line... If only I can get my friends to lower me down to see him... If only I can touch the side of his cloak...* For Bartimaeus it was *If only I can get his attention...so I'll stand up and scream.*

You may not have everything that other people have, things like money, success, pedigree, friends, family or health. You have to use what you do have, and one of the things everyone can have is faith. That's what Bartimaeus, the man on the roof and the woman with the issue of blood all had in common. Bartimaeus' faith was manifest in his voice and his movement. He dropped his cup, stood up and, with the little bit of faith he had, he screamed.

Faith may at times sound difficult to grasp, but at its simplest form, faith is seeing Jesus for who he is and keeping your eyes on him. And how about learning that from a blind guy? He cannot see anything, but he sees Jesus for who he is, and that's the key to his miracle.

If you get caught up in what people think, then that will be a rope-line between you and your breakthrough.
If you get caught up in your circumstances, then that

will be a rope-line between you and your breakthrough.

Your age doesn't define you. Your circumstances don't define you. Your past doesn't define you. Your image doesn't define you. You are defined by what God says about you and you need look no further than Jesus to find out what that is. Jesus says that you are chosen. Jesus says that you're an heir, just like him. Jesus says that you're more than a conqueror. Jesus says that you can do all things through Christ who gives you strength.

If you can see Jesus for who he is, you'll see yourself for who you really are. That's when you have faith that brings a breakthrough in your life. God wants to move you from begging with a cup to abundant living. From spiritual blindness to seeing the possibilities you were designed for, God wants to move you from where you are to where you want to be. The key that unlocks this is faith–seeing Jesus for who he really is.

If you can stand up and scream, then you are on your way to blessing the blessing and breakthrough that you need. If you believe enough about Jesus to jump the rope-line, Jesus believes enough about you to provide you a breakthrough.

Key Thought
If you believe enough about Jesus to jump the rope-line, Jesus believes enough about you to provide you a breakthrough.

Questions for Reflection

When have you felt that you were behind a rope-line trying to get to Jesus?

Not only did Bartimaeus stand up and scream, but another man was lowered by his friends to Jesus and a woman touched the edge of his cloak. These were all examples of taking a radical posture to express belief in Jesus. What is a radical posture that you can take to do the same?

PM

Read the other two rope-line stories in Mark 2:1-12 and Mark 5:21-34. What encourages your faith from these stories?

_____

_____

_____

_____

_____

_____

_____

_____

_____

_____

_____

_____

_____

_____

_____

Notes

Day 7:
LORD HAVE MERCY

The Word

Then they came to Jericho. As Jesus and his disciples, together with a large crowd, were leaving the city, a blind man, Bartimaeus, was sitting by the roadside begging. When he heard that it was Jesus of Nazareth, he began to shout, "Jesus, Son of David, have mercy on me!" Many rebuked him and told him to be quiet, but he shouted all the more, "Son of David, have mercy on me!" - Mark 10:46-48

Daily Dose

When Bartimaeus cries out for mercy, it is simply a cry for help. If you think about it, that's about all we should be doing when we ask God for help. He already knows everything, including the truth about our motives, our real needs, or what we've been feeling as we go through something. He knows what's best for us and what He is accomplishing in our lives. But God also knows the truths we don't know, which could include why something happened, what other people were thinking and doing, and even what the outcome is going to be. I don't think Bartimaeus was some kind of theologian, but he does give us a theologically sound way to ask for help: just say "Lord, have mercy." Go ahead, give it a try right now.

Mercy is one of the most essential qualities of God (Ex 34:6, 7; Dt 4:31; Mi 7:18–20). It reveals His character. Specifically, it talks about the quality in God by which he faithfully keeps his promises and maintains his relationship with his people despite our unworthiness and unfaithfulness (Dt 30:1–6; Is 14:1; Ez 39:25–29; Rom 9:15, 16, 23; 11:32; Eph 2:4). Prominent in the concept of mercy is the compassionate posture to forgive an offender or adversary and to help or spare him in his sorry plight.

The biblical meaning of mercy is rich and complicated, as evidenced by the fact that several Hebrew and Greek words are used in the Bible to describe it, giving us many synonyms in the Bible translations including: "kindness," "lovingkindness," "goodness," "grace," "favor," "pity," "compassion," and "steadfast love." At the heart of all of these concepts of mercy is the love of God, which is freely given in his gracious saving acts to those he is in relationship with, regardless of what they've done or their present condition.

Let me drop a quick Bible study on ya:

In the Old Testament, God persistently puts up with his disobedient and wayward people and continuously seeks them out to draw them back to himself. The psalmist describes God as a father who pities his children who reverence and trust him (Ps 103:13). Hosea pictures God as a loving father who looks down from heaven with a yearning heart of compassion upon his rebellious and wayward people (Hos. 11). He also regards Israel as an unfaithful and adulterous wife whom God loves as a faithful husband in spite of her apostate and sinful condition (Hos. 1–3). Isaiah depicts God as a mother who has compassion on the son of her womb (Is 49:15).

These pictures reveal God's mercy in rich and different ways. Other dimensions include forgiveness and restoration to favor, and deliverance from distress and perils. Because of what Israel as a nation had learned about the steadfast love and faithfulness of God, devout Jews instinctively lifted their voices in petition for divine mercy and forgiveness in times of need, eloquently expressed in the penitential psalms (Ps 6; 32; 38; 51; 102; 130; 143) as well as other OT passages (Ex 34:6; Neh 9:17; Ps 57; 79; 86; 123; Is 33:1–6; Dn 9:3–19; Jl 2:13). It is the remembrance of God's mercy that gives the repentant person the hope and assurance of divine favor and of reconciliation with the offended Lord.

This is precisely what Bartimaeus was doing–following in a long line of God's people who knew, based on history and the character of their God, that if they would use their voice to cry for mercy, God would hear their prayers.

Later in the New Testament we see that the real mercy is not the healing of blindness or any of the other healings where Jesus answered a cry for mercy. Rather, the ultimate mercy is God's provision of salvation for mankind in Jesus Christ (Rom 11:30–32; Eph 2:4). God is "the Father of mercies" (2 Cor 1:3) which he gives to those who believe in his Son. It is because he is "so rich in mercy" that he saved those spiritually dead and doomed by their sins–"only by his undeserved favor have we ever been saved...all because of what Christ Jesus did" (Eph 2:4–6). It is out of God's mercy that one is forgiven and granted eternal life (1 Tm 1:13–16).

Key Thought

If we use our voice to cry for mercy, God will hear and deliver us.

Questions for Reflection

Where do you need mercy in your life right now? This is a place where you may feel unworthy or unfaithful, where you feel a need of deliverance or compassion from God, or a place where you need favor or reconciliation.

PM

There was a significant amount of Scripture in today's Lord Have Mercy devotional. Take some time to read through some of those passages, highlighting and underlining those that address your situation specifically.

Notes

Chapter 2
DROP YOUR COAT

Day 8:
JESUS STOPS

The Word

Jesus stopped and said, "Call him."
So they called to the blind man, "Cheer up! On your feet! He's calling you." Throwing his cloak aside, he jumped to his feet and came to Jesus.
- Mark 10:49-50

When Jesus came down from the mountainside, large crowds followed him. A man with leprosy came and knelt before him and said, "Lord, if you are willing, you can make me clean." Jesus reached out his hand and touched the man. "I am willing," he said. "Be clean!" Immediately he was cleansed of his leprosy...

When Jesus had entered Capernaum, a centurion came to him, asking for help. "Lord," he said, "my servant lies at home paralyzed, suffering terribly."

Jesus said to him, "Shall I come and heal him?" The centurion replied, "Lord, I do not deserve to have you come under my roof. But just say the word, and my servant will be healed. For I myself am a man under authority, with soldiers under me. I tell this one, 'Go,' and he goes; and that one, 'Come,' and he comes. I say to my servant, 'Do this,' and he does it." When Jesus heard this, he was amazed and said to those following him, "Truly I tell you, I have not found anyone in Israel with such great faith... Then Jesus said to the centurion, "Go! Let it be done just as you believed it would." And his servant was healed at that moment.

When Jesus came into Peter's house, he saw Peter's mother-in-law lying in bed with a fever. He touched her hand and the fever left her, and she got up and began to wait on him.
When evening came, many who were demon-possessed were brought to him, and he drove out the spirits with a word and healed all the sick. - Matthew 8:1-16

Daily Dose

I run my own business, which at times is awesome because I am my own boss, the chief architect of results for the company and my clients. It allows me to fulfill my life mission of H.O.W.: "Helping Others Win." Of course, one of the personal perks is that I own my schedule as well as getting to travel to some of the most amazing places in the world. My work travel coupled with my family's love for vacations is a perfect match. When my sons were about 9 and 13, our family went on vacation to Universal Studios and Disney.

My wife and boys love rides like roller-coasters and other adrenaline pushers that appear to be fun from a distance. I know it may seem fun to them, and maybe even to you, but I absolutely can't stand any rides of any sort. I'm not a Negative-Nancy-Doubting-Thomas-No-Fun-Rev-Run type of guy–I just get sick on any type of ride. Even a simulator ride will have me sick for days and nearly ruin our vacation because I get sick, and my family gets sick of me. (I know that was a lot of sickness in one sentence but I wanted you to get the point.) My agreement with my family is: "You guys have fun. I love you and I will happily and patiently wait on you while I have my own fun with a funnel cake."

On this particular Disney trip, my boys started to interrupt my chilling and relaxing all-cool time at the Happiest Place on Earth. They began nagging me to join them for at least one ride. I kept saying no and they kept trying to make their lame dad feel bad. After what must have been the tenth interruption, I gave in simply because they had exhausted me. I rode not only one ride but several, simply for my sons' pleasure. By the looks on their faces, their enjoyment was running loop-da-loops like my belly. But you know what? I enjoyed it too–so much that our new vacation tradition at amusement parks is for dad to ride a few rides and the family to get a kick out of it. If you ask my boys their favorite part of a family vacation, they will probably say it's getting dad on a couple roller-coasters.

What started as an annoying interruption from my sons has turned into an amazing opportunity to make them happy. There have been plenty of times as a father that I've turned away the interruptions–that day, I did it nine times before giving in! But now I try to allow some interruptions from my kids and see if they contain some unknown pleasure that I cannot foresee.

Did you know this is how our heavenly Father is with us? God loves our interruptions. And we see this perfectly in Jesus.

Although it's grown on me when it comes to my kids and family, for the most part interruptions are still somewhat difficult for me. I sometimes wish I could just hang a little "Do Not Disturb" sign around my neck, like I usually hang up on my hotel room door. When I'm busy, which is often, I like to really focus on what I'm doing. But I can't just tune out the rest of the world because I believe God wants me model his character–to be ready for interruptions.

Jesus was not only constantly being interrupted, but he made Himself interruptible.

Directly after the transfiguration in Matthew 8, where Jesus was revealed in his divine glory to three disciples, he immediately descends the mountain to the valley where "large crowds" are pulsing to interrupt his mountaintop experience. Matthew paints a picture of four interruptions, all in succession. A leper asks for and receives healing. A Roman centurion asks if his servant can be healed. Peter drags Jesus to his mother-in-law's house to heal from the edge of death. (I guess he liked his mother-in-law!) The chapter ends with a description of "many" who were brought to him with demon-possession as well as healing "all" who were sick.

People just came up to Jesus with every problem they had. If you read all four Gospels, it just goes on and on. What does that say about God? What does that reveal about his priorities?

Jesus stops.
God loves our interruptions.
You are his priority.

Key Thought

Jesus loves our interruptions. We are always his priority.

Questions for Reflection

When was the last time you interrupted God for something? What is something going on in your life right now that you have not yet brought to God because you feared he wouldn't be available?

PM

Read the Scriptures that are from Matthew 8 where Jesus is interrupted several times. Write in your journal or Bible what this reveals about the character of God.

Notes

Day 9:
JESUS CALLS

The Word

Jesus stopped and said, "Call him."
So they called to the blind man, "Cheer up! On your feet! He's calling you." Throwing his cloak aside, he jumped to his feet and came to Jesus.
- Mark 10:49-50

As Jesus started on his way, a man ran up to him and fell on his knees before him. "Good teacher," he asked, "what must I do to inherit eternal life?"
"Why do you call me good?" Jesus answered. "No one is good–except God alone. You know the commandments: 'You shall not murder, you shall not commit adultery, you shall not steal, you shall not give false testimony, you shall not defraud, honor your father and mother.'"
"Teacher," he declared, "all these I have kept since I was a boy."
Jesus looked at him and loved him. "One thing you lack," he said. "Go, sell everything you have and give to the poor, and you will have treasure in heaven. Then come, follow me."
At this the man's face fell. He went away sad, because he had great wealth.
Jesus looked around and said to his disciples, "How hard it is for the rich to enter the kingdom of God!"
The disciples were amazed at his words. But Jesus said again, "Children, how hard it is to enter the kingdom of God! It is easier for a camel to go through the eye of a needle than for someone who is rich to enter the kingdom of God."

The disciples were even more amazed, and said to each other, "Who then can be saved?"

Jesus looked at them and said, "With man this is impossible, but not with God; all things are possible with God."

Then Peter spoke up, "We have left everything to follow you!"

"Truly I tell you," Jesus replied, "no one who has left home or brothers or sisters or mother or father or children or fields for me and the gospel will fail to receive a hundred times as much in this present age: homes, brothers, sisters, mothers, children and fields–along with persecutions–and in the age to come eternal life. But many who are first will be last, and the last first." - Mark 10:17-30

Daily Dose

Jesus stops and calls the blind man.

What does it mean to be called? If it means being called to a profession, I've had lots of callings over the course of my life.

I went to college with a vague "call" to become an attorney because all of my young life, people told me that I could argue with the best of them. Shortly after arriving to college I realized that I liked mentoring the underserved and underprivileged kids, so I pivoted to counseling and social work through my undergraduate years. I went on to a masters degree in criminal justice management and administration with hopes to work in the corrections field. I believed I was "called" to be a shining light while people were in their darkest places.

For over 12 years I worked in the fields of corrections and criminal justice in some capacity; when I was 25, I ended up becoming one of the youngest prison wardens in the country!

Then I felt like God was "calling" me to leave my comfortable, secure and amazing job in corrections to start a consulting company and lobbying firm. Not only was I going to help other correctional agencies around the country improve their operations and outcomes, but I wanted to help influence policies and politics for the better. I had this burning desire to run for state office and be the next JC Watts, who was the first black Republican congressman from the state of Oklahoma.

On my road to political office, I felt "called" to do more with the church our family was attending. I ended up becoming a campus pastor, launched a location from construction to nearly 4,000 people in over four years and was able to be a part of seeing countless lives transformed, marriages restored, hopes enlarged, dreams awaked and stories resurrected. Those five plus years of pastoring were some of the most defining of my adult life–our family was clicking, my leadership capacity was increasing and my God-given potential was intensifying. I went hard in the paint. (Translation for non-basketball fans: "I worked hard and gave it all that I had" for 5 years.)

During that time, I felt "called" to confront the three areas that we "are not supposed to talk about": Race, Religion, and Politics. So, I wrote a book called *Church Diversity–Sunday The Most Segregated Day Of The Week*. I began speaking at various churches about that book, all while still Pastor at LifeChurch. Eventually, I felt "called" to step out and share this message more broadly. That's when I started NxtLevel Solutions, my consulting and strategy firm where we work with some of the most amazing churches, nonprofits and corporations around the world. I write books, travel, speak, and help individuals and organizations tap into the depths of their greatness and realize their potential. Simply put, we partner with people to help them get to their next level of influence.

After nearly a half dozen "callings" I've stopped using that word, because my calling has never changed. I have been called to serve Jesus and bring him glory—it's only my jobs that have changed. I think when calling appears some 700 times in the Bible, it's usually not taking about what we "do" for work. Most often in the New Testament, the word for calling is the Greek word *klesis*, and it refers not to our secondary callings of vocation, but our primary calling to Christ. As someone else has said, we are called to someone before we are called to something or somewhere. We are called to Christ before we are called to become a social worker, a warden, a politician, a pastor, an author, a consultant or to Oklahoma or South Africa or West Palm Beach.

What you do most of the day doesn't define you any more than blindness defined Bartimaeus. What defined him was that he was called by Jesus Christ, and it wasn't about a job. Bartimaeus responds to the call of Christ, but the preceding story in the Bible is the so-called rich young ruler, who does the opposite—he rejects the call of Christ. Immediately after the rejection, the disciples ask Jesus who can be saved, and directly after Jesus answers, he saves Bartimaeus.

This isn't an accident–Jesus' action is continuing the lesson he began in words. The one who is saved is anyone who cries out like this guy. Jesus is always calling and always speaking.

Here are two important questions:

- Are you listening for and answering the call, or are you hanging up the "do not disturb" sign?
- Do we realize who the caller is and what he has called us to?

If you need a refresher on that, short of reading the entire Bible, you can just tweet, text or write this to yourself every day:

But you are a chosen race, a royal priesthood, a holy nation, a people for his own possession, that you may proclaim the excellencies of him who called you out of darkness into his marvelous light. Once you were not a people, but now you are God's people; once you had not received mercy, but now you have received mercy.[i]

Key Thought
We are called to Christ before we are called to become anything.

Questions for Reflection

How have you responded to the call of Christ on your life? Are you listening for and answering the call, or are you flipping to "do not disturb"? Do you realize who the caller is and what he has called you to?

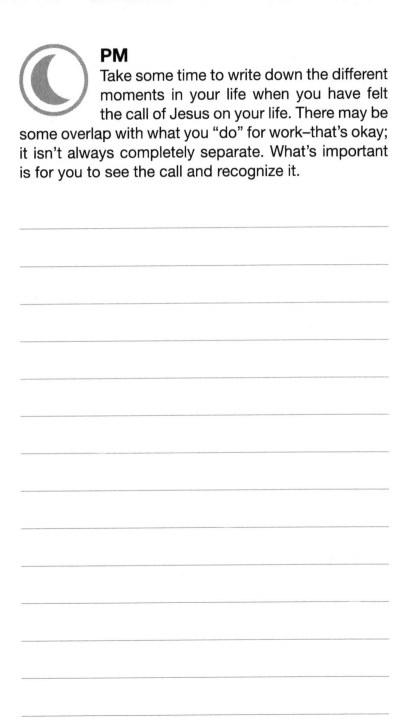

PM
Take some time to write down the different moments in your life when you have felt the call of Jesus on your life. There may be some overlap with what you "do" for work–that's okay; it isn't always completely separate. What's important is for you to see the call and recognize it.

Notes

Day 10:
CHEER UP

The Word

Jesus stopped and said, "Call him."
So they called to the blind man, "Cheer up! On
your feet! He's calling you." Throwing his cloak
aside, he jumped to his feet and came to Jesus.
- Mark 10:49-50

Daily Dose

Jesus stops His journey and issues a command to the crowd–"Call him."

Remember, there was a huge crowd throbbing as they surrounded Jesus. He was throwing around healing like a NFL rookie throws around cash, and the entourage was growing. But in the order of those who were important enough to be around Jesus, the blind like Bartimaeus were at the bottom of the ladder. They certainly were not part of the entourage. He was so socially insignificant that the crowd and Jesus' entourage (the disciples) sternly rebuke Bartimaeus to remain quiet. But then everything changes because the caller speaks a calling to the one at the margins!

The crowd responds appropriately, "Take heart; rise, he is calling you." Jesus has always known Bartimaeus, always loved him and always called him. The crowd has avoided Bartimaeus, pushed him to the margins and told him to shut up. But when Jesus calls us, Jesus defines us. This is why some in the crowd recognize that this is a significant turn of events for someone like Bartimaeus and tell him to cheer up at the possibility of a new life through the call of Jesus.

The phrase "cheer up" comes from the Greek word *tharseo*, which literally means "take courage." I think of an old pirate movie or something where some swashbuckler tells the young kid about to get killed to "take courage, old chap."

But Jesus actually uses this word quite a bit, and it's not used by him in death scenes to convey a cheap encouragement that will end with death by a sword.

He uses it to convey certain hope at the coming life transformation. We see this with the healing the paralytic on the mat[ii], healing the woman with bleeding[iii], calming the disciples' fears as he walks on the water[iv], comforting his disciples with the promise of the peace of the Holy Spirit and the promise that he has overcome the world[v], and a promise to Paul that he will not die but will take the Gospel to Rome[vi]. The words for "cheer up" or "take courage" almost always precedes not only a miracle, but both peace and astonishment.

Indeed for Bartimaeus. He comes expecting to receive what he believes Jesus, the Son of David, can provide–mercy and healing. I don't imagine they needed to tell him to cheer up and take courage–it's almost as if they were trying to get on the right side of the miracle, instead of being the crowd yelling him down. The reality is that they were just "fans," cheering and booing as a crowd, similar to how similar crowds would cheer and boo Jesus days apart on Palm Sunday and Good Friday. We humans are fickle, and the only person in this story consistently devoted to responding to the call of Jesus was Bartimaeus. He comes across as the hero and like all good hero stories, he gets recognized for his audacious and tenacious cries for mercy.

When Jesus calls us, no matter our position, the call holds a certain hope of coming life transformation. The only uncertainty about the call is if we will expect to receive what is promised.

Key Thought
When Jesus calls us, Jesus defines us.

Questions for Reflection

What is a place in your life where you need Jesus to speak a word of courage and certain hope to you? How can you search for those words–in the Scriptures, from other Christians, through prayer?

PM
Based on your answer to the reflection question, take a moment to search for God's defining call in your life—a word of courage or hope that you desperately need.

Notes

Day 11:
ON YOUR FEET

The Word

Jesus stopped and said, "Call him."
So they called to the blind man, "Cheer up! On
your feet! He's calling you." Throwing his cloak
aside, he jumped to his feet and came to Jesus.
- Mark 10:49-50

Daily Dose

My family loves sports and in particular, there are two teams that we fanatically follow: the NBA's Oklahoma City Thunder and the University of Oklahoma (OU) Sooners. This past year, I had the opportunity to conduct chapel for the Sooners Football team in their last home game of a Final Four season. Needless to say, I was as pumped as a linebacker who sees the quarterback move out of the pocket. (For my friends on the other side of the pond, insert your favorite Rugby or Soccer illustration here.) I was also excited to be able to bring my youngest son, Jayden. At just 12 years old, he was easily the biggest fan in our house. He knew every player—their position, strengths, weaknesses and things that only coaches would know. As we were going into chapel, his eyes dilated with excitement as he got to see his favorite players up close and personal. Not only was he a fan, but he was hoping to accomplish a life mission–play for OU and the NFL.

Of course, he was strutting into the team hotel with an OU sign, OU hat, OU sweatshirt and a Sharpie just in case he could get in position to get an autograph. Shortly after we arrived the Chaplain informed us that the players don't generally do autographs at chapel.

I'm not saying my son was heartbroken, but I'm sure his heart had a few hairline fractures.

Once it was my turn to deliver the chapel message I stepped up and delivered a very poignant message about David and Goliath and looked directly into the eyes of every coach, player, parent, recruit and staff member. I looked into their eyes and spoke directly to their hearts. After the message, the players and coaches all seemed to be jacked up in a good way. My son got to see his dad as a hero in front of his hero OU players. After I finished speaking Jayden came up to the front with me as almost every player, recruit and coach came up to say "thanks" and "that's what I needed," shook my hand, give me some dap and the bro hug. To top it off the players and coaches were talking to him, shaking his hand and giving him the official "what's up lil' man" head nod. Jayden is a lil' guy because he's only 12, but he's built like a linebacker, fullback and running back all in one. You can look at him and say "He's a football player."

As most of the players were through the line and on to the game, THE CLIMAX of Jayden's young life happened. Head coach Bob Stoops came up, asked him his name, what school he went to, what position he played and grabbed him by the shoulders and said "You're awful solid for a 12-year-old. I'm going to have to keep an eye out for you."

Day made. Drop the mic. Shut the door. Pleasantly plump lady can start warming up her vocal cords because "It's Over."

Usually, when you get in line for autographs with

celebrities, there's a rope-line—a zone you have to stay in, a place you belong, that sets you apart as not being like the person on the other side of the rope-line. That morning as we prepared for chapel, Jayden was expecting the rope-line; maybe if he was lucky he would get that autograph, and he sure he was disappointed to not get one. But Jayden jumped the rope-line and got into the players' pre-game meal area and film room located at their team hotel. Who needs an autograph when God gave him an upgrade of stature to remember from the head coach of his favorite team, of his favorite sport in the world? He stood tall and proud for quite a while on that moment.

What would make you stand up proud?

What would make you rise to your feet and jump a rope-line?

Bartimaeus is behind his own rope-line. He is sequestered away from those allowed to be close to Jesus. He's so far away from Jesus that he has to shout and scream, without being able to see him because of the crowd. The crowd is loud and boisterous, all clamoring for the first century version of an autograph: a touch of the edge of Jesus' cloak, maybe a conversation, maybe a dramatic healing. Bartimaeus didn't have this privilege. But then suddenly Bartimaeus is thrust past the rope-line for a face to face encounter with Jesus.

Bartimaeus could have refused. He could have made the excuse that his obstacles were too great, his condition too elapsed, his position too marginal. But he stood up and got to his feet and jumped that rope-line.

Standing up to jump the rope-line means putting yourself in the right place at the right time for the right interaction with Jesus. His desire is to overcome your real obstacles through a real encounter. And sometimes the best way to set us up for that is to put us behind the rope-line. Then we know what it really means to get that access when Jesus calls.

Often the major life change we seek requires personal hardship, sorrow, mistreatment, or suffering, and that's mainly because most of us won't escape life without those realities. When walking through difficult things, we think we are on the other side of the rope-line from God, and discouragement sets in: "I'm not getting that autograph today." But then the miracle begins, first by being willing to humble ourselves and resist the naysaying and control of others, then by putting ourselves in the right place at the right time.

When Jesus calls, Bartimaeus comes in spite of the obstacles! He throws off his cloak and although he cannot see, he jumps the rope-line between him and Jesus. He gets on his feet and fights history, the crowd and what everyone else thinks is proper.

Jesus doesn't care about proper; he cares about people. I like to say it this way: "Great leadership is always less about the leader and more about the ship." Yes, Jesus is always concerned about the ship and that ship includes you and I. It includes all of us willing to be in the boat. And when one of his people is ready and willing to put themselves in position for healing, blessing and breakthrough, Jesus is gonna pull a Coach Bob Stoops every time!

Key Thought
Jesus doesn't care about proper; he cares about people, and when you are willing to put yourself in a position to meet him, he will always show up.

Questions for Reflection

What would it look like for you to change your position and get in a better place to experience and meet with God?

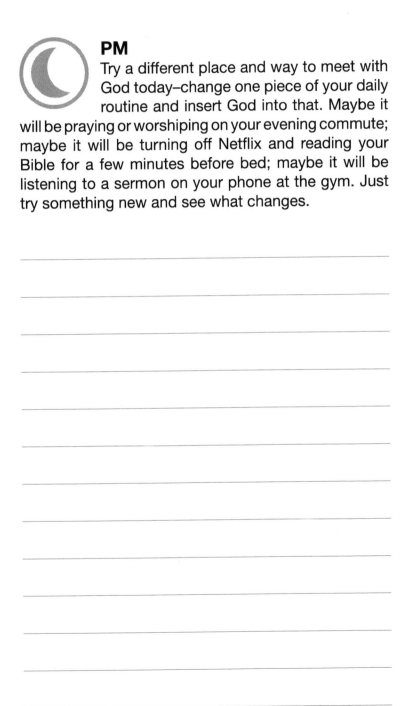

PM

Try a different place and way to meet with God today—change one piece of your daily routine and insert God into that. Maybe it will be praying or worshiping on your evening commute; maybe it will be turning off Netflix and reading your Bible for a few minutes before bed; maybe it will be listening to a sermon on your phone at the gym. Just try something new and see what changes.

Notes

Day 12:
THROWING THE CLOAK

The Word

Jesus stopped and said, "Call him."
So they called to the blind man, "Cheer up! On
your feet! He's calling you." Throwing his cloak
aside, he jumped to his feet and came to Jesus.
- Mark 10:49-50

Daily Dose

Storytelling expert Robert McKee talks often in his screenwriting seminars about an "inciting incident," an event that radically upsets the balance of forces in the protagonist's life. It is an event that provokes a desire in the protagonist that he must satisfy, or forces the character to take action in pursuit of a goal. McKee argues that a protagonist's desire is to bring their life back into balance. Sometimes an inciting incident can be negative like a kidnapping, a job loss or a serious illness, but other times it can be positive, like winning the lottery, getting a promotion or a near death experience. Without an inciting incident, the character will not change, move forward or take action in pursuit of a goal, because there is nothing to provoke them.

Bartimaeus needed an inciting incident to provoke him to action, and all it took was Jesus. The balance of his life had been steady–put on his cloak, beg outside the temple, go home–every single day. But this day was different, so when he heard that Jesus had called him, he knew it was his chance. It was enough to provoke him to not only stand up, but to throw aside his cloak.

What is the cloak? Begging was an occupation that

required going to the town elders and proving that they were either physically disabled or poor with no family ties. The elders would then give them a special color coat that would signify to the town that they were a beggar. The cloak, though a gift, became an identity marker–a uniform of his need. He would wear the cloak and sometimes even spread it out in front of himself to receive whatever gifts a passerby was willing to toss his way. If his coat was stolen, he would be unable to continue begging until it was replaced. It was his source of comfort and even provided the security of having been approved by the city elders.

When Jesus asks if the man really wants to be healed, it means that immediately, in order to be healed, he must throw down his coat–his occupation, security and comfort. Bartimaeus' response was dramatic and decisive as he cast aside his cloak, sprang to his feet and stood before Jesus with nothing.

Our cloak is a symbol for the balance of our lives, and sometimes we need an inciting incident to cause us to throw off our cloak, to get us off balance. If you are a workaholic, an inciting incident would be your kid looking you in the eye and asking "can you spend more time with me?" If you are lacking a prayer life, an inciting incident would be a job loss or a sudden illness that drops you to your knees. We don't get to choose our inciting incidents; they choose us, it seems. Really, it's the providence of God at work. Whether the inciting incidents are positive or negative in nature, the intent is that we throw aside that which protects–our identity uniform, our comfort, our security–and leap to our feet, abandoning balance to respond to the call of Jesus. When we throw down our cloak in pursuit of what God has for us, we are positively advancing in the faith.

If you are having trouble throwing down a cloak right now, perhaps it's important to remember that it only appears to protect, identify and comfort you. Once you see that illusion for the mirage that it is, you'll stop running at breakneck speed toward a desert watering hole that isn't there. Like Jesus providing water welling up to eternal life to a thirsty woman at midday, only God can provide the protection, identity and comfort that we crave. Protection, identity and comfort are not garments we wear and wrap ourselves in. They are realities we receive through the grace of God. And all he asks is that we throw that cloak down.

 Key Thought
Protection, identity and comfort are not garments we wear and wrap ourselves in. They are realities we receive through the grace of God.

Questions for Reflection

What has been an inciting incident in your life? How did it provoke you?

PM

Draw a straight horizontal line. Put a dot halfway. Write the words "inciting incident" and write what your most recent one was (we will have many over the course of our lives). To the right of those words, above the line write the things you have learned because of it, and below the line write the things that have been a challenge because of it.

Notes

Day 13:
THE CLOAK OF COMFORT

The Word

Jesus stopped and said, "Call him."
So they called to the blind man, "Cheer up! On your feet! He's calling you." Throwing his cloak aside, he jumped to his feet and came to Jesus.
- Mark 10:49-50

I have learned to be content whatever the circumstances. I know what it is to be in need, and I know what it is to have plenty. I have learned the secret of being content in any and every situation, whether well fed or hungry, whether living in plenty or in want. - Philippians 4:11-12

Daily Dose

Everyone has seen the movie *The Blindside*. (And if you haven't, you need to watch it tonight before you complete another day of this devotional. I'll wait here…)

One of the more defining moments in the movie was a scene that played out when Big Mike came to live with the Tuohys. Leigh Anne Tuohy looks at Big Mike as she is setting him up in his room at their home, and he has this amazed look on his face. Leigh Anne reads it as a potential problem with the room and she asks, "What's the matter?" Michael replies, "I've never had one before." "What you've never had your own room before?" Leigh Anne questions. Michael replies, "No, a bed."

I don't generally cry during movies, but *Blindside*

definitely had some tearjerker moments. Speaking of tearjerkers, my wife, on the other hand, cries quite often in movies. When I feel a tearjerker moment is happening, I simply focus my attention on LaKendria because I know she will be shedding some tears.

My wife and I have been on mission trips around the world and we have seen people the same age as us and our children without running water, clean water, electricity, and even without beds. The amount of money we spent on our flight to get to them on our trip would have changed the life of that family for a year, probably providing food for every day or a modern home. Such an experience of our comfort up against their destitution breaks our hearts. After such experiences, you would have to be the coldest human being alive to not appreciate even the smallest of amenities that we are blessed with in our lives regularly. That *Blindside* moment about the bed really blindsided me; it made me realize that you don't have to go around the world to find people without. It was also a great reminder that life is all viewed through a lens we call perspective, as long as we choose to put on the glasses of honesty.

Years ago, I had a moment where I got honest with myself. I realized I was complaining about how slow the Internet was while I was traveling on a plane. I thought to myself, "Really Scott? You are complaining about Internet not being up to your standard while you are flying 36,000 feet across the country in your designer clothing? Please, shut your privileged mouth." Now, as do many, I call that #FirstWorldProblems–we have to keep our complaints in context or not complain at all.

Blind Bartimaeus didn't have first world problems; in fact, quite the opposite. But while he did have a certain level of comfort in his status as a beggar, he was willing to make a fool of himself shouting for Jesus to help him as he dropped his coat. Dropping our cloak of comfort means standing out and exposing ourselves as being people in need. It creates a vulnerability that previously we would have found impossible and gets us one step closer to true contentment, a destination that is guarded by our own pride as much as it's developed by our own humility. This, I believe, was Apostle Paul's secret of being content:

I have learned to be content whatever the circumstances. I know what it is to be in need, and I know what it is to have plenty. I have learned the secret of being content in any and every situation, whether well fed or hungry, whether living in plenty or in want.

Paul has had all the ups and downs of provision, security and comfort, but he has also discovered that contentment has nothing to do with those. Contentment has to do with crucifying our crippling pride, recognizing the provision, security and comfort that God provides to us. All while being completely faithful and trustworthy in his ability to do so. The Bible presents people over and over who are to be admired for their faithfulness to God expressed in their trust of him as they left their comfort zones. Whether it was a difficult conversation, a geographical move, a bold prophecy, a ridiculous prayer, or a plea for a miracle, the characters change but the truth doesn't.

As a consultant with clients all around the world, I find

myself in airplanes often. As a result of me flying so much, I generally get upgraded to first class where the people that you meet can be very interesting. When I begin to have a conversation with my seat mate, people always ask, "What do you do for a living?" When I reply that I'm a pastor, the conversation changes quickly as people begin stuffing their liquor bottles in the seatbacks in front of them and ladies try to cover up their *50 Shades of Gray* books with magazines.

One time I was sitting by a guy in first class and we began to talk about social media as I was streaming live on Periscope. He began to ask me questions about it, and of course he popped the question, "What do you do for a living?" Of course I reciprocated and asked him what he did for a living. His response: "The Global Brand Director at Nike." I know it's not just me, but what goes through your mind when you are sitting next to the global brand director at Nike? "Hook a brotha up with some shoes!" I didn't actually say it, but there is a 100% chance that I thought it.

As we began to talk about his journey and how he got his current position, he told me about a time that he was at dinner with a large group of friends. He said he began to take stock of his life and what he was doing or not doing with it. He realized that he had become complacent and comfortable, so he began applying for various positions. He ended up with this amazing job at Nike.

The moral of the story isn't the fact that he got an awesome job at Nike; the moral of the story is that if he didn't get out of his comfort zone and "Drop His Coat" he would have never been in a position to experience an amazing opportunity and an amazing breakthrough.

When we drop the coat of comfort, God picks us up and does some incredible things. Think of Joseph and his brothers. Think of Abraham leaving his city. They both received something wildly beyond their ability to ask or imagine. Think also of Jonah, or the rich young ruler we talked about yesterday, or the Global Brand Director for Nike. Their unwillingness to be uncomfortable led to their unwillingness to be a part of God's ultimate plan for their lives.

If we can drop the cloak of comfort, God can provide beyond our wildest dreams. When we clutch the cloak, God will be forced by our choice to clutch it right back, and that's not a place any of us ever want to be.

Key Thought
When we drop our coat of comfort, God comforts us and picks us up.

Questions for Reflection

What is an area of your life that you have grown comfortable? What would it tangibly mean for you to drop that area and be content instead?

PM
Read Paul's secret of being content in Philippians 4:11-12. What is God saying to you through this passage? What would it look like for you to practice contentment?

Notes

Day 14:
GOOD COMPANY

The Word

Jesus stopped and said, "Call him."
So they called to the blind man, "Cheer up! On your feet! He's calling you." Throwing his cloak aside, he jumped to his feet and came to Jesus. - Mark 10:49-50

A friend loves at all times, and a brother is born for adversity. - Proverbs 17:17

Iron sharpens iron, and one man sharpens another. - Proverbs 27:17

A man of many companions may come to ruin, but there is a friend who sticks closer than a brother. Proverbs 18:24

Faithful are the wounds of a friend; profuse are the kisses of an enemy... Oil and perfume make the heart glad, and the sweetness of a friend comes from his earnest counsel. - Proverbs 27:6, 9

Do not be deceived: "Bad company ruins good morals." - 1 Corinthians 15:33

Daily Dose

As a dad, I'm always keeping an eye on the types of friends my boys are hanging out with. This has been going on since preschool. There have been times where I've wanted them to spend less time with some and more time with others, but as a parent, that is something difficult to control. Nothing makes us feel more helpless than being able to see a friendship turning sour or, even worse, toxic, and feeling like we cannot get them to see it. Sometimes those premonitions turn out to be prophecies, and I have to help them pick up the pieces from a friendship that hurt them or get them back on the right path from the bad influence of a friend. Of course, I'm not an expert on friendship, but I know its value.

Mike is one of my best friends in the world, and it's been that way since college. He stood next to me when I made my vows and is a guy who knows everything about me and vice-versa. Some years back, Mike and I had a disagreement over something, and I'm not even going to give you the details because now it seems trivial. It was a serious enough disagreement that we didn't talk for a couple of years. It was sad, but it was also a busy time of life with plenty to focus on, so my posture could be summed up with the words: "Oh well." It wasn't right, but I just moved on until God starting challenging me that it was a relationship I needed to restore.

The longer we stayed disconnected, the more I appreciated the relationship that we had. I'm not exactly sure how it happened but I remember it was orchestrated by God. We reconnected and it was almost like we never missed a beat.

God gives us relationships for a reason. Some relationships are seasonal and others are a lifetime, and for me, it took distance and a severed relationship to realize the importance of keeping your great friends close and your loved ones even closer.

There's no shortage of wisdom about friendship in the Scriptures. Proverbs tells us that we need good friends to help us through adversity, to sharpen us, to stick close when nobody else will, to drive faithfulness and blessing in our lives, and to help us do what is right, growing in integrity and the character of God. You show me a young Christian man or woman with ungodly friendships, and I'll show you a young Christian who is in serious spiritual trouble. Based on my years in the prison system and my years pastoring in churches (which, by the way, are really not that different), I can tell you unequivocally that as the friends go, so goes the man or woman.

We are unsure of the makeup of Bartimaeus' circle of acquaintances and friends. He could have had great fellowship with fellow beggars or he could have had a godly family that supported him. Or he could be at the other end of the spectrum, lonely or surrounded by what Proverbs calls "bad company." What we do know about Bartimaeus' company is important for all of us to learn.

There are two groups of influence in this story, and Bartimaeus can gravitate or listen to either of them, but not both. One group is made up of those who told him to shut up—we talked about them last week as haters, and indeed they are. They are pushing him back from Jesus, not encouraging him closer.

The other group in the story are those who told Bartimaeus to get up, encouraging him, egging him on, pushing him closer to Jesus and closer to something that they may not even get to experience themselves. They are selfless friends.

Of course, the crowds probably weren't that black and white for Bartimaeus, with people who were one second telling him to shut up and the next moment telling him to cheer up. People are fickle, then as now. There will always be people who push us closer to Jesus, people who push us further from Jesus, and some we can't figure out how they fit in. But this isn't about the people. It's about Bartimaeus–it's about who he listens to!

What we need in our life is people who help us hear the call of Jesus. We need the opposite of haters: lovers. People who truly love us and help us love Jesus better. If you don't gather good company around you and follow the wisdom of Proverbs, you'll gravitate towards listening to the ever-loud voices that cut you down, curse your beliefs, and corner your faith. If people put you on the defensive about Jesus, put yourself on the defensive from that friendship. If people help you approach closer to Jesus, approach them and ask to spend more time together. If your kids aren't choosing friends well, check your own example first, and then make sure you are one of their greatest spiritual friends. If God has gifted you with a lifelong friendship but you've allowed the enemy to sever it, then allow God to restore it.

Key Thought
We need people in our lives who help us hear the call of Jesus.

Questions for Reflection

Think or look back over the people you have spent time with over the last week. Without judgment, which of them are haters and which of them are lovers? Who are you giving more influence in your life?

PM

Who is one person that truly loves you and helps you love Jesus better? How can you make it possible for them to influence you more significantly in the next 30 days? Get creative, and then do it. Make the invitation!

Notes

Chapter 3
DROP YOUR CUP

Day 15:
DO YOU KNOW?

The Word

"What do you want me to do for you?" Jesus asked him.

The blind man said, "Rabbi, I want to see."

"Go," said Jesus, "your faith has healed you." Immediately he received his sight and followed Jesus along the road. - Mark 10:51-52

Now the serpent was more crafty than any of the wild animals the Lord God had made. He said to the woman, "Did God really say, 'You must not eat from any tree in the garden'?" The woman said to the serpent, "We may eat fruit from the trees in the garden, but God did say, 'You must not eat fruit from the tree that is in the middle of the garden, and you must not touch it, or you will die.' "

"You will not certainly die," the serpent said to the woman. "For God knows that when you eat from it your eyes will be opened, and you will be like God, knowing good and evil."

When the woman saw that the fruit of the tree was good for food and pleasing to the eye, and also desirable for gaining wisdom, she took some and ate it. She also gave some to her husband, who was with her, and he ate it. Then the eyes of both of them were opened, and they realized they were naked; so they sewed fig leaves together and made coverings for themselves.

Then the man and his wife heard the sound of the Lord God as he was walking in the garden in the cool of the day, and they hid from the Lord God among the trees of the garden. But the

**Lord God called to the man, "Where are you?"
He answered, "I heard you in the garden, and I
was afraid because I was naked; so I hid."
And he said, "Who told you that you were naked?
Have you eaten from the tree that I commanded
you not to eat from?" - Genesis 3:1-11**

Daily Dose

Do you know what you need?

For most of us, it's difficult to separate what we actually
need from what we really just want. If we are honest,
the things that we want reveal some of the idols of our
hearts. We often clutch and worship things like money,
sex, power and possessions.

Now, if Jesus personally had a conversation with me
and asked me, like he did Bartimaeus – "What do
you want me to do for you?" – I am pretty confident
I wouldn't tell him something related to an idol in my
life. I'm guessing you wouldn't, either.

But what would I answer? I'm not sure I know. Do you?
Do you know what you need?

This is a fascinating detail about the Bartimaeus story:
God knows exactly what Bartimaeus needs, why he is
shouting and why he is pursuing him. But God makes
Bartimaeus articulate it! Why? Is this some kind of
healing game or magical formula? Well, no. Jesus
doesn't always have people tell him their needs before
he heals them. But Bartimaeus has to express his
need to Jesus in order to unlock his miracle, and also
in order to teach us a lesson.

Too often our admiration for Jesus is a vague attraction, but Jesus wants our fullest attention combined with the self-examination necessary to know that *HE* is necessary. Bartimaeus knew precisely what he wanted: his sight. Knowing what we need involves the one thing that so many of us wish to face: our deficits.

Where do we fall short?
What is holding us back in life?
What secret does God already know but we keep trying to hide from him?

So many of us are still hiding in a garden, covering ourselves up with leaves. Meanwhile God is still in relationship with us, asking us to come out of hiding—a ridiculous charade if ever there was one because God knows where we are, anyway. He just wants us to recognize that we are hiding.

Bartimaeus's eyes could not physically see Jesus, but Bartimaeus' faith could spiritually see Jesus for who he was. He drops his cup because he realizes that money isn't what he needs. What he needs is healing, and so he starts pursuing Jesus for what he really needs. When he gets asked the question, he isn't telling Jesus he needs some loose change or a home or a job or anything else that would be a common answer from a beggar. He's desperate for healing and that's exactly how he answers Jesus' question.

When we go to Jesus, if we are as desperate and as definitive as Bartimaeus, things will happen. We need Jesus to do something for us, and the only prerequisite is an answer to his question: "What do you want me to do for you?"

This is the most important question God ever asks us, and the one to which we most frequently give the wrong answer. Our answer to this question will reveal whether we want death or life, whether we want to be healed from our blindness or selfishly want to use God to do our bidding and fulfill our own desires.

We often ask for all the wrong things in life, focusing on the things we can see and touch. The harsh reality is the most important things in life generally aren't things. Maybe we should take a lesson from the blind man's book and stop focusing on what we can see, do some serious self-examination, and start giving a great answer to Jesus' question.

Each of us will have different answers, but they are all rooted in the same ministry of Jesus. He's about restoring what's been lost, and he can and will, if we ask him.

Key Thought

Too often our admiration for Jesus is a vague attraction, but Jesus wants our fullest attention combined with the self-examination necessary to know that HE is necessary.

Questions for Reflection
What do you need?

PM

As if Jesus has just asked you, write your answer to "What do you need?" in the form of a letter to him. Concentrate on not writing anything that you want or even idols; just focus on what you need. You might want to answer these questions as a way to get at the real answers of what you need:

- Where do you fall short?
- What is holding you back in life?
- What secret does God already know but you keep trying to hide from him?

Notes

Day 16:
FAITH

The Word

"What do you want me to do for you?" Jesus asked him.
The blind man said, "Rabbi, I want to see."
"Go," said Jesus, "your faith has healed you." Immediately he received his sight and followed Jesus along the road. - Mark 10:51-52

Now faith is confidence in what we hope for and assurance about what we do not see. This is what the ancients were commended for. - Hebrews 11:1

Daily Dose

Faith still moves mountains and we've still got mountains to move. But do we have the faith that will move them? Bartimaeus did. His faith, though small and simple, was exceptional and because of his faith, Bartimaeus was commended by Jesus. This follows the pattern of others in the Scriptures were commended for their faith, with perhaps the best example being the so-called "Hall of Faith" in Hebrews 11.

Here comes another quick Bible lesson:

The phrase Jesus used to commend Bartimaeus was "your faith has healed you." In the original Greek language of the Bible, the phrase is just the word for "faith" followed by one word to convey "has made you well." In secular Greek literature, "has made you well" means to be saved and delivered from a particularly perilous situation or mortal danger–things like salvation from war, shipwrecks, drowning, being thrown from a chariot or a difficult desert crossing. But the most common use in secular Greek is medical–being healed from a disease. In fact, doctors and physicians were called "saviors."

In the Bible, these uses are maintained, but the meaning focuses to describe a person either being saved, restored, or delivered from an illness or securing their place in heaven/eternity. Some of the uses of the word are not just examples, but quick and deep lessons on faith:

- When God promises a son to Mary, the angel uses this phrase to describe how the son's name Jesus will be fulfilled by "saving" the people from their sins.[vii]
- Peter uses it to cry out to Jesus to "save" him when he is sinking.[viii]
- The woman who reaches for Jesus' cloak guesses that if she touches his garment, she will be "saved." Jesus then uses the word to commend her faith that has "made her well."[ix]
- Jesus uses the word to say that if we try to "save" ourselves, we won't.[x]
- Jesus uses the word to defend his healing a man on the Sabbath because it is lawful to "save" life.[xi]
- Jairus uses the word in his plea for Jesus to heal his daughter, when he expresses faith that Jesus alone can save her.[xii]
- Mark tells us in his Gospel about Jesus that anyone who simply touched just the fringe of Jesus' clothing were "made well."[xiii]
- Jesus makes certain claims about himself

that he is the door through which people are "saved."xiv

Why did I just walk you through that Bible study on being made well? Because most of us need to be reminded of what faith looks like in action. Most Christians believe God is able and that our faith is necessary, but most Christians cannot point to a recent time in their lives when they were "saved" or "made well." Maybe this says more about our faith than it does about God's willingness or power to save! God is not the one in question; we are. And the question is simple: how big is our faith?

God is not moved by the size of your situation; God is moved by the size of your faith. What appears to be small when firmly planted with belief will grow and can move mountains. "Yet when planted, it grows and becomes the largest of all garden plants, with such big branches that the birds can perch in its shade." Mark 4:32 We talked about shade in previous days; I love that the Scripture outlines the fact that the bird can perch in its shade. With a strong faith you can handle the shade and you can press towards your destiny. Having a strong faith won't remove your problems; however, it will remove their power and influence over your life.

When we drop our cup, we pick up faith. Those who walk in faith, like in the examples above, the examples that make up the entire eleventh chapter of Hebrews and those in Bartimaeus' story, discover that there is no place in our lives where God lacks the ability to save, restore or deliver. He's bigger than the mountains we want to move. So if we want to move a mountain,

we should do what God told us to do: express faith–
tell that mountain to move.

Remember: **God is not moved by the size of our situation; God is moved by the size of our faith.**

Key Thought

God is not moved by the size of our situation; God is moved by the size of our faith.

Questions for Reflection

How big is your faith? Can you remember a time when your faith was expressed in a way where God undoubtedly responded to your faith by acting according to his nature as a Savior?

_____

_____

_____

_____

_____

_____

_____

_____

_____

_____

_____

_____

_____

_____

PM

There were eight passages above that were given to show you Bartimaeus' type faith in action. Read as many as you have time for, and write down in a journal or in your Bible margins what you learn about faith.

Notes

Day 17:
IMMEDIATELY

The Word

"What do you want me to do for you?" Jesus asked him.
The blind man said, "Rabbi, I want to see."
"Go," said Jesus, "your faith has healed you." Immediately he received his sight and followed Jesus along the road. - Mark 10:51-52

As they were walking along the road, a man said to him, "I will follow you wherever you go."
Jesus replied, "Foxes have dens and birds have nests, but the Son of Man has no place to lay his head."
He said to another man, "Follow me."
But he replied, "Lord, first let me go and bury my father."
Jesus said to him, "Let the dead bury their own dead, but you go and proclaim the kingdom of God."
Still another said, "I will follow you, Lord; but first let me go back and say goodbye to my family."
Jesus replied, "No one who puts a hand to the plow and looks back is fit for service in the kingdom of God." - Luke 9:57-62

Daily Dose

Immediately Bartimaeus responds to the call, leaps to his feet, drops his cup and abandons his cloak. Bartimaeus responds to Jesus dramatically and decisively, casting aside his outer garment, springs up to his feet and seizes his moment with Jesus. The response of Jesus is no less swift, immediately healing him.

The word "immediately" in the original language of the Bible conveys a straight pathway—the shortest distance between two points. It's a word used to describe travel or a pilgrimage, much like the one the crowds are on as Bartimaeus is begging along the way. But in the Bible, the word also becomes a favorite description for both *Jesus' urgency in his mission and the urgency expected on the part of disciples*. Of the 70-plus uses of the word in the Gospels, the author Mark uses nearly half of them.

Why? Mark is concerned to show the urgency with which people pursue Jesus as well as the immediate response of a God who is also pursuing the people!

In Bartimaeus' case, he brings nothing to Jesus but himself, but what he does bring, he brings urgently and decisively. He comes expecting to receive what he believes Jesus, whom he calls the Son of David, can provide: mercy and healing. When Bartimaeus hears the call of Jesus, he drops his cup immediately. Certain opportunities in life only happen once. Bartimaeus instinctively knew that.

This is not how most people respond to the call of Jesus. Some hear the call of Christ and decide to wait until they are at another spot in their life, until they have all the answers, or until responding is more convenient. Jesus in fact teaches about this as he interacts with three prospective disciples, all of which decide that they are going to pass on the opportunity to follow

Jesus. The passage, which you can read above, seems harsh on the surface, potentially revealing a God who seems fickle or disingenuous in his offer to follow him. But what is actually happening is Jesus responding to our tendency to be unlike Bartimaeus and respond slowly to his call.

In the first encounter, we meet a rash disciple. Crowds often flocked to Jesus out of impulse instead of conviction. Like crowds today gathered around a celebrity or waiting to get their new iPhone, they are riveted, charmed, smitten, emotional, and enthusiastic. After feeling all the feels, this disciple is compelled to tell Jesus that he will go anywhere with him. Jesus wants him to weigh the real nature and strength of his attachment to Christ; if he does, he is welcome. But Jesus isn't out for fans. He's looking for disciples.

In the second encounter, we meet a procrastinating disciple. He is willing but not yet ready, even though he is called instead of offering like the first case. Most likely, this situation was one where a son has an aging father who doesn't have many days left, and the son believes it's his duty to take care of him. But Jesus tells him that there are two kingdoms. Under this harsh-seeming surface, Jesus is teaching him that God's Kingdom lies neglected, which is why Jesus has called the man to be a disciple and lead in his Kingdom, something required of all disciples. Jesus goes on to tell him that in the other kingdom, the world, his father will indeed die, but he will not be neglected. Jesus is telling him "I need you to get in the game and stop neglecting my work. Fewer are qualified and called–I have qualified and called YOU. Others are qualified to care for your father."

In the final encounter, we meet a wavering disciple. He volunteers BUT. He is sort of a combination of the first two encounters, wanting to press pause on his response and "say goodbye" to his family. He does not have in mind a quick goodbye, nor does he have in mind the seriousness of Jesus' call. Based on the warning of looking back, it is clear his discipleship is not yet thorough and his separation from the world is not complete. His allegiances, comforts and conveniences are pulling his look backwards, away from his forward call to Jesus. This is not a case of going back but of looking back, which is why Jesus references Lot's wife[xv] in another similar story. It's not the actual return to the world but a reluctance to break with it. Plowing requires an intent eye, and a straight row is destroyed the instant one turns.

The whole point of the three encounters with Jesus are the same point as Mark's insistence in the Bartimaeus story and his Gospel on "immediately."

We have to seize our moment of invitation when Jesus gives it. If you want to experience breakthrough, it's going to require some breaking.

If you want to be healed immediately, you have to drop your cup immediately.

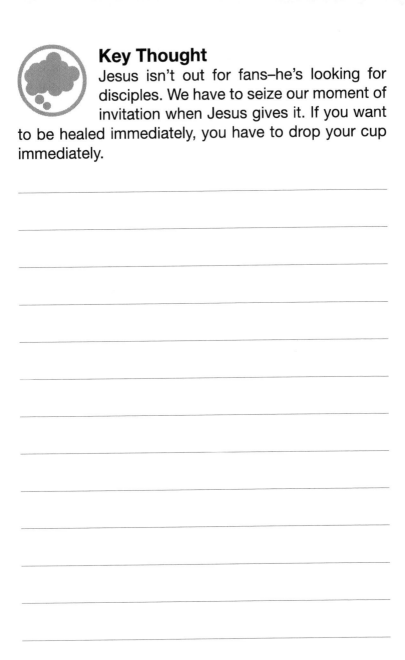

Key Thought

Jesus isn't out for fans—he's looking for disciples. We have to seize our moment of invitation when Jesus gives it. If you want to be healed immediately, you have to drop your cup immediately.

Questions for Reflection

What has God invited or asked you to do that you have been slow to respond?

PM

Read the Luke 9 passage above one more time. This time, try to diagnose which one of the three responses to Jesus is most like you!

Notes

Day 18:
VOICES

The Word

> "What do you want me to do for you?" Jesus asked him.
> The blind man said, "Rabbi, I want to see."
> "Go," said Jesus, "your faith has healed you." Immediately he received his sight and followed Jesus along the road. - Mark 10:51-52

Daily Dose

In professional sports, there is a big difference between being a home team and a visiting team, but in certain cities with certain sports, the home crowd is more hostile to the visiting team than others. We live in Oklahoma City and are proud fans of the Oklahoma City Thunder, our franchise NBA team. My family loves going to the games, cheering for the Thunder; more often than not, on our home court the outcome is generally in our favor with a "W." The Thunder crowds are known for their passion and fire, rivaling what might be seen in home games for the Duke Blue Devils or other well-known college basketball home courts. The entire crowd stands up until the first bucket is made; we have a section in the upper level that has been given the name "loud city;" overall, we are just a radical bunch that loves cheering on our team. It's always funny to watch opposing fans in the OKC Thunder Chesapeake Arena attempt to cheer, scream and root on their team, only to be silenced by the hostile, rowdy and passionate OKC Thunder fans. Thunder fans absolutely love the cheering, screaming and yelling—it's the reason we would rather be there than in our living room or at a bar watching the game. And the opposing fans? They cower down in their seats and usually become invisible, or at least quiet. The stars on the opposing team are used to it, learning to not be deterred by the voices and focus on their game. I'm always amazed at how they can hit that foul shot despite the deafening sounds and distracting fans.

In the same way that the dominant voices usually win out in an arena, the dominant voices usually win out in our lives, unless we can learn to tune them out and play our game.

For Bartimaeus, whether it was the insults of the crowd or the yells to be quiet, he was focused on hitting his shot—in his case, dropping his cup and getting in front of Jesus. He refused to be deterred and in fact, the louder they cried out, the louder he cried out, insisting with his faith that he be heard. He may have had to cast off every last bit of his dignity, but he wasn't pushed off his goal.

When Jesus calls, there are voices that try to determine our response. And it always seems like we have to follow Jesus rather than the crowd. Sometimes choosing to focus on the call of Jesus means standing alone, and the crowd can feel pretty hostile! In the story, Bartimaeus is not merely isolated and alone. He is going against the currents of the many so he can meet the One.

Let me get real with you for a second by asking a question that you are welcome to lie about, but I'd recommend you take a moment to be honest: What are the other voices that you listen to and are capturing your attention?

One set of voices is rooted in our own a lack of discernment, failing to recognize the potentially dangerous voices in your life. Be careful! The voices that deter us aren't always obvious, like the hateful yelling around Bartimaeus. They are more like the slithering snake in the Garden, deceiving, telling us something our itching ears want to hear. The latest self help book, Dr. Phil, Dr. Oz or Dr. Oprah, and even advice from others can fall into this category.

The other set of voices are often temptation. Think of Jesus in the garden–all three temptations were bathed in Scripture to make it seem more appealing, but it was still just temptation to do what's wrong.

There are other voices in our life holding us back, but the point is this: we are either seeking after hearing from God or we are seeking after hearing from those voices.

Bartimaeus went against the crowd because of his extreme desperation, need, and certainty that Jesus was the one who could do something about it. He was utterly determined to meet the one person whom he longed to confront with his trouble. In the mind of Bartimaeus there was not just a vague, wistful, sentimental wish to see Jesus. It was a desperate desire, and it is that desperate desire that gets things done. When asked to be silent, he cries out all the more. Bartimaeus continues to cry out his profession of faith, with even greater enthusiasm and energy.

When the voices tempt you to silence and exhaustion, find some strength and cry out all the louder.

Key Thought

In the same way that the dominant voices usually win out in an arena, the dominant voices usually win out in our lives, unless we can learn to tune them out and play our game.

Questions for Reflection

We either seeking after hearing from God or we are seeking after hearing from the voices of others. How have you seen each play out in your life recently? Where have you had victory in hearing God's voice over the voice of others?

_____

_____

_____

_____

_____

_____

_____

_____

_____

_____

_____

_____

_____

_____

PM

Take some time to identify a voice that you often have to tune out, but struggle to do so. Why does this voice have power over you? How can you silence or ignore that voice in your life? Are there any immediate steps you can take?

Notes

Day 19:
DOGGED DETERMINATION

The Word

"What do you want me to do for you?" Jesus asked him.
The blind man said, "Rabbi, I want to see."
"Go," said Jesus, "your faith has healed you." Immediately he received his sight and followed Jesus along the road. - Mark 10:51-52

Five times I received at the hands of the Jews the forty lashes less one. Three times I was beaten with rods. Once I was stoned. Three times I was shipwrecked; a night and a day I was adrift at sea; on frequent journeys, in danger from rivers, danger from robbers, danger from my own people, danger from Gentiles, danger in the city, danger in the wilderness, danger at sea, danger from false brothers; in toil and hardship, through many a sleepless night, in hunger and thirst, often without food, in cold and exposure. And, apart from other things, there is the daily pressure on me of my anxiety for all the churches. - 2 Cor. 11:24-29

Daily Dose

If you were guaranteed success at the end of a difficult task, would you be more or less engaged, resolved or committed? Whether it's a football team that can smell the championship, a difficult marriage that can sense redemption is around the corner, an arduous climb up a mountain that glimpses the last steep hill or a small business that's finally getting some traction, our resolve and commitment increases exponentially when we believe we are going to accomplish what we've set out to do.

It's interesting that we learn as much about people in the Gospels as we do about Jesus. For example, people are presented throughout Mark's Gospel as examples of what can only be described as dogged determination–a resolve and commitment to, in their case, experience Jesus. The Gospel opens with an untouchable leper who doggedly pursues Jesus for a healing touch, when both a divine healing and human touches unthinkable for his disease (Mark 1:40-45). Several friends must force their way through a crowd and through a roof to lower their paralyzed companion to Jesus[xvi]. A woman with the flow of blood must disregard laws that forbid her from having contact with Jesus, presses through a pulsing crowd and extends her arm to touch the edge of his garments in order to receive his help[xvii]. Her story is immediately followed by that of Jairus who must ignore the mockery of the crowd, pleading with Jesus to heal his dead daughter despite the finality of death and his servant urging him to come back home for the funeral[xviii]. A desperate father must overcome his doubt that Jesus can do anything to help his tormented son when the disciples have already failed[xix]. And of course there is Bartimaeus, persistently pleading for Jesus to intercede in his life.

There is no doubt that in each case of need, the people about to interact with Jesus have envisioned a future reality where their situation is better. They envision healing, freedom, deliverance and life. And no doubt they have tried other ways of getting there. But they have heard enough to ignite a spark of belief that Jesus could bring the transformation they seek–that somehow he could right all the wrongs.

Indeed, Jesus is willing to heal those who are resolved and committed; it seems to be an evidence of true faith and belief in him. Healing comes to those who are persistent and are not quickly discouraged by whatever hurdles are placed in their way. They set their sights on the reality they believe God has for them through Jesus Christ, and they just keep trudging on, waiting for their opportunity to express that faith in a cry or plea.

Perhaps the most important factor of having such resolve and commitment is not losing sight of Jesus in the midst of what you're going through.

I sometimes have to remind myself of the life of the Apostle Paul. Are you aware of the list of perils he went through in just about twelve or so years after his transformative experience with the risen Christ? Paul was put through the wringer:

> **Five times I received at the hands of the Jews the forty lashes less one. Three times I was beaten with rods. Once I was stoned. Three times I was shipwrecked; a night and a day I was adrift at sea; on frequent journeys, in danger from rivers, danger from robbers, danger from my own people, danger from Gentiles, danger in the city, danger in the wilderness, danger at sea, danger from false brothers; in toil and hardship, through many a sleepless night, in hunger and thirst, often without food, in cold and exposure. And, apart from other things, there is the daily pressure on me of my anxiety**

for all the churches.

Paul, despite lashing, beatings, stoning, shipwrecks, multiple "dangers," physical needs and even the brutality of leading the churches, Paul never wavers in his resolve and commitment to pursue and advance the mission of Jesus, nor does he lose his faith and belief that God will continue to deliver him and the church according to his plans. This dogged determination carries from Mark's characters through Paul to become a defining characteristic of the early church.

Is it still true of us today? Are we so desperate for a vision to come to pass that we will just keep trudging forward in faith? Can our resolve and commitment be easily shaken by our own versions of beatings and shipwrecks?

Key Thought
Our resolve and commitment increase exponentially when we believe we are going to accomplish what we've set out to do.

Questions for Reflection

If Paul's determination is a 10 and complete and utter lack of motivation is a 0, what number would you give to your determination and why?

_____

_____

_____

_____

_____

_____

_____

_____

_____

_____

_____

_____

_____

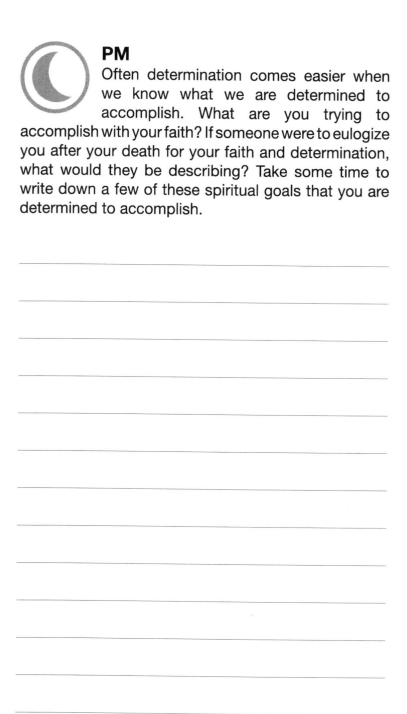

PM

Often determination comes easier when we know what we are determined to accomplish. What are you trying to accomplish with your faith? If someone were to eulogize you after your death for your faith and determination, what would they be describing? Take some time to write down a few of these spiritual goals that you are determined to accomplish.

Notes

Day 20:
DON'T HESITATE TO DROP IT

The Word

> "What do you want me to do for you?" Jesus asked him.
> The blind man said, "Rabbi, I want to see."
> "Go," said Jesus, "your faith has healed you." Immediately he received his sight and followed Jesus along the road. - Mark 10:51-52

Daily Dose

What have you dropped?

If you've gotten this far in this devotional, hopefully you've taken advantage of it! We've talked about dropping our care, our coat and our cup, and I've encouraged you to do so immediately.

In our story, Bartimaeus cannot hesitate, thinking, "Maybe I will wait until Jesus passes this way again in a less crowded, less hectic time." Those who are healed in the Gospel of Mark act decisively and throw pride and caution to the wind to seize the one chance they get when Jesus passes by. Otherwise, the opportunity for salvation, restoration and deliverance will be lost.

One of the most resounding messages of the first chapter of Mark is: don't miss Jesus! He gives us a shotgun approach of character introduction, revealing a myriad of people who meet and interact with Jesus, most of whom feel a sense of urgency, mirroring Jesus' own urgency at getting on with his mission.

In the first chapter of Mark, there is an extended story

of John the Baptist pointing the way to Jesus. Then, in quick succession, Jesus calls his first disciples along the sea of Galilee, drives a demon out of a man in Capernaum, heals Simon's mother-in-law as well as the whole town gathered, and heals a man born with leprosy. The people come out of the woodwork to meet him, bring him themselves and others who need salvation, restoration and deliverance. More than once Mark comments about how quickly the news of Jesus was spreading through the region.

Hesitation and delay is a clear mark of those who see did not recognize Jesus as the son of David, the Messiah. Often it manifests by people's questions and excuses, but it also appears in stories of contrast where one person sees Jesus for who he is and responds, while many do not. Sometimes the many grow violent, sometimes they shoo Jesus out of town and sometimes they just stand dumbfounded as Jesus performs the miracle for the one despite the hesitation of the many.

The irony in the Bartimaeus story is clear: Bartimaeus, a blind man, "sees" Jesus as the Son of David, while the crowd and the religious leaders fail to see him as such. Those who have faith in Jesus see the truth and do not hesitate to activate their faith for what they need. Those who do not, hesitate.

Delay and hesitation in the Scriptures is not a positive trait. Whether it is a delay in reaching a decision or a reluctance to reach a decision on account of uncertainty, caution or rebellion, Scripture provides examples of individuals who hesitate in the face of divine commands or promises, and indicates the

dangers of delay:
- Lot and his wife [xx]
- Moses [xxi]
- Peter [xxii]
- Israel during the Exodus [xxiii]
- Gideon [xxiv]
- Israel during the time of Elijah [xxv]
- Jeremiah [xxvi]

Scripture also provides the example of people who did not hesitate, and goes on to directly tell us to never do so:
- Caleb [xxvii]
- Simon and Andrew [xxviii]
- Paul [xxix]
- Do not hesitate to speak [xxx]
- Jesus Christ commands immediate obedience [xxxi]

I could keep going on with positives and negatives, but you get the point! When Jesus calls, we must not hesitate to drop whatever is keeping us from fully following him. If we are hesitating, it's because we are uncertain about who he is, disobedient to what he's asked or struggling with the priority of where he is in our lives.

It's a good practice in our relationship with Jesus to invite him to confront us on our hesitations every now and then. Ask God what you've been avoiding, how you've walked in uncertainty, where you are being disobedient and where your priorities are out of line. If your life is anything like mine, you'll get plenty of answers every time!

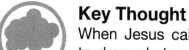

Key Thought

When Jesus calls, we must not hesitate to drop whatever is keeping us from fully following him. If we are hesitating, it's because we are uncertain about who he is, disobedient to what he's asked, or struggling with the priority of where he is in our lives.

Questions for Reflection

Is there anything God has told you to do during this devotional that you have hesitated to do? What has held you back? What do you need to move forward?

PM

Read the positive and negative examples of hesitation above. Use this as encouragement to set out and accomplish what you have been hesitating to do.

Notes

Day 21:
ON THE WAY

The Word

"What do you want me to do for you?" Jesus asked him.
The blind man said, "Rabbi, I want to see."
"Go," said Jesus, "your faith has healed you." Immediately he received his sight and followed Jesus along the road. - Mark 10:51-52

But this I confess to you, that according to the Way, which they call a sect, I worship the God of our fathers, believing everything laid down by the Law and written in the Prophets, - Acts 24:14

Therefore, the wicked will not stand in the judgment,
nor sinners in the congregation of the righteous;
for the Lord knows the way of the righteous,
but the way of the wicked will perish. - Psalm 1:5-6

Daily Dose

One of the earliest names for the Christian community, even used by the Apostle Paul himself, was "the Way." First used in Acts 9:2, it was apparently used by both the Jewish and the secular community and appeared in both positive and negative assessments of the church.[xxxii] Paul's use of the term begins when he is seeking to kill Christians but eventually, as his own life is on the line, he employs it in his defense before Felix, suggesting that the name had at least quasi-official acceptance as Felix is said to have heard and known about "the way" (24:14, 22).

In the Old Testament, the word "way" was frequently used metaphorically to refer to human behavior, usually to contrast those who had fallen into sin and those who had not—the "good way"[xxxiii] and the "evil way."[xxxiv] "Way" is also frequently used to designate the ethical guidelines which God set forth for his people[xxxv], and this "way" is distinguished from man's way, which inevitably leads him to sin.

Blind Bartimaeus' story begins with him sitting along the way, and by the end of the story he is on the way with Jesus. Blind Bartimaeus leaves all, comes to Jesus and receives sight. He then follows Jesus on the way toward Jerusalem. This isn't just wordplay; it's significant. According to the use of the word in the Scriptures, plus what we know of Jesus himself, this was an about-face for Bartimaeus—one that many others, including the Apostle Paul, would experience. Truly, Jesus is the only one who can place someone on the way with him, but when we allow it, we will be changed because it's *the way* God has always intended for his people.

Bartimaeus was stuck before he encountered Jesus and after the encounter he was moving with him. This is how life change happens! It doesn't come because you see Jesus coming; lots of crowds saw Jesus. But only a handful experienced the life change that Bartimaeus did. Life change comes not because you see Jesus coming and wait for him, but because you see Jesus coming and jump up to seize your encounter. When God interrupts you, don't hesitate. Interrupt God back. Don't give up because people throw shade or shout you down.

And once you are on the way with Jesus, don't let anyone cut in on you, shove you off the way, or put distance between you and the God you are walking behind. Cut the strings to the things that try to negatively control your life. Keep Changing and keep growing.

Key Thought
Once you are on the way with Jesus, don't let anyone cut in on you, shove you off the way, or put distance between you and the God you are following.

Questions for Reflection

We are left hanging with Bartimaeus' story, left to assume that the change he began to experience in this encounter continued on the way with Jesus throughout his life. Five years from now, how will the encounter you've had with Jesus the last three weeks still be changing you? Is there anything you can do to solidify that change?

PM
Read the Scriptures footnoted above about "the way," both good and bad. Make a list or circle in your Bible the characteristics of those who are on the way of Jesus.

Notes

AFTERWORD

The most important lesson we can learn from the life of Bartimaeus and his encounter with Jesus is this:

You need to drop all of the stuff that you are holding onto in order to grab hold of the things that God has for you. You need to cut the strings to the things that control your life. Don't get so caught up in your situation, problems, shortcomings and setbacks that you lose sight of what Jesus can and will do immediately in your life. What appears to be a setback is often times a set-up for your success.

Maybe, just maybe, Jesus is saying to you and me:

"I have something amazing for you and I want to put it into your hands, but I can't give it to you because your hands are full holding onto all of the unnecessary stuff of the past and present..." You need to drop some stuff from this season in order to grab hold of what God has for you in the new season.

Drop It and live a life of faith and victory instead of fear and failure.

ENDNOTES

i. 1 Peter 2:9–10
ii. Matthew 9:2
iii. Matthew 9:22
iv. Matthew 14:27
v. John 16:33
vi. Acts 23:11
vii. Matthew 1:21
viii. Matthew 14:30
ix. Matthew 9:21-22
x. Matthew 16:25
xi. Mark 3:4
xii. Mark 5:23
xiii. Mark 6:56
xiv. John 10:9
xv. Luke 17:32
xvi. Mark 2:1-12
xvii. Mark 5:25-34
xviii. Mark 5:35-43
xix. Mark 9:14-26
xx. Genesis 19:16, 26; Luke 17:32
xxi. Exodus 3:11,13; 4:1,10,13; 6:12
xxii. Acts 11:12 See also Acts 10:14-20
xxiii. Numbers 13:31-33; 14:1-4
xxiv. Judges 6:36-40
xxv. 1 Kings 18:21
xxvi. Jeremiah 1:6
xxvii. Numbers 13:30
xxviii. Mark 1:16-18
xxix. Acts 20:20, 27
xxx. Isaiah 58:1
xxxi. Luke 9:62
xxxii. See Acts 19:9, 23; 22:4; 24:14, 22
xxxiii. Psalm 1:6; Proverb 8:20; 12:15, 28
xxxiv. Psalm 1:6; 119:101, 104, 128
xxxv. Genesis 18:19; Exodus 18:20; 32:8; Deuteronomy 8:6; 26:17
xxxvi. Judges 2:19; Job 22:15; Proverbs 12:15; 16:2

ABOUT THE AUTHOR

Scott Williams is an author, speaker, strategist and international consultant. As the Chief Solutions Officer of NxtLevel Solutions, Scott and his team consult with some the largest and most influential churches, nonprofits, and Fortune 500 companies in the world in guiding them to solutions that instill leadership and foster growth.

Prior to his founding of NxtLevel Solutions, Scott served as one of the key leaders and Campus Pastors at Life.Church (formerly LifeChurch.tv), which is the largest and one of the most innovative churches in America. Additionally, Scott has been featured on several prominent "best of" lists in some of the nation's most respected publications. Those lists include being number five on the Top 100 Christian Leaders to Follow, Top 25 Diversity Professionals, Top 30 Leadership Blogs, Top 15 Leadership Experts, Top 100 Employee Engagement Experts and Top 500 CEO's in The World.

Previously, Scott served in various leadership roles as a lobbyist, political consultant, college professor, leadership consultant, strategist and various other influential roles. Scott's extensive experience with church growth, leadership development, technology, marketing, organizational health and being a serial entrepreneur makes him a true asset to organizations across a breadth of industries.

Scott is sought after speaker, leadership engineer, diversity expert and strategic consultant. He has been dubbed as, "The Strategy Doctor" by various industry leaders. He is the author of several books: "Church Diversity, Go Big, Drop It and 16 Great Ways To Come Up With Great Ideas."

Scott lives in Oklahoma City with his wife LaKendria and two sons Wesley and Jayden. He and his family are proud fans and supporters of their home team, The Oklahoma City Thunder.

SCOTT WILLIAMS
Stay Connected:

- @ScottWilliams
- @ScottWilliams
- @ScottOKC
- @ScottOKC

DROP IT

Made in the USA
Charleston, SC
04 June 2016